Languages of Sydney: The People and the Passion

By Alice Chik, Susan Markose and Diane Alperstein

Candlin & Mynard ePublishing
Hong Kong

Published by Candlin & Mynard ePublishing Limited
Unit 1002 Unicorn Trade Centre
127-131 Des Voeux Road Central
Hong Kong

ISBN: 9780463438664

Languages of Sydney: The people and the passion
Copyright 2018 by Alice Chik, Susan Markose and Diane Alperstein

Candlin & Mynard ePublishing Limited was founded in 2012 and is incorporated as a limited company in Hong Kong (1830010). For further information, please see the website: http://www.candlinandmynard.com

Cover image: Provided by the authors

This book is copyright material and may not be copied, reproduced, printed, distributed, transferred or used in any way that contravenes the relevant copyright law without written permission from the publishers.

All copyright royalty is donated to *The Australian Literacy & Numeracy Foundation* (https://alnf.org/). The Foundation focuses on raising literacy levels in Australia's most marginalised communities, including the refugee and Indigenous communities. We hope you will support us by buying a paper or hard back copy.

LIST OF FIGURES

1. Barbara
2. Tina
3. Munira
4. Amy
5. Atfah
6. Zebadiyah
7. Zinovia
8. Mark
9. Olivia
10. Zeel
11. Sofia
12. Janice
13. Ella
14. Lily
15. Raaina
16. Deanne
17. Dustan
18. Pareesa
19. Jack
20. Jayden
21. Saiqa
22. Aayah
23. Sehrish
24. Ava
25. Sally
26. Caleb
27. Elaine
28. Samuel
29. Sona
30. Esther
31. James
32. Theresa
33. Linda
34. Agatha
35. Helen
36. Katarina
37. Dan
38. Paul
39. Philip
40. Sevinc
41. Tham
42. Samantha
43. Hasna
44. Shanu
45. Cherry
46. Nafiye
47. Andrew
48. Hamayoon
49. Stella
50. Mafalda
51. Emilia
52. Judy
53. Alexis
54. Pompiliu
55. Maggie
56. Frank
57. Eliza
58. Daniel
59. Branca
60. Rita
61. Madeline
62. Neil
63. Diah
64. Simon
65. Matthew
66. Chivy

CONTENTS

Acknowledgements — 1

About the authors / contributors — 2

Foreword — 5
by Terry Lamb

Chapter 1 — 9
Introduction

Chapter 2 — 12
The languages, the people, the passion

Chapter 3 — 148
How children depict their multilingual selves?
From a research goal to the Heritage Language classroom
... and back! A research memoir
by Sílvia Melo-Pfeifer

Appendix — 157
A blank portrait

Index of keywords — 158

ACKNOWLEDGEMENTS

The authors of this work are all migrants who have brought with us to our home in Australia, the languages and cultural heritages of our countries – Alice and her Chinese, Susan and the diverse languages of her heritage, and Di's background in multiple South African languages. At some point in our lives, we have tried learning different languages, with varying degrees of success and frustration. As educators, our work involves working with languages and literacy. We are surrounded by languages.

We would like to thank Macquarie University's initial teacher education students for their generous sharing of their language portrait silhouettes and narratives. We could not have produced this book without their contribution. We would also like to thank Professor Terry Lamb, University of Westminster, for his insightful sharing of experiences and advice during the initial conceptualization of this volume and the foreword he has written for the book. His excitement and enthusiasm, both reflected in his personal observations and his ability to see the significance of this research, have inspired us. Special thanks to Prof Dr Sílvia Melo-Pfeifer, Universität Hamburg, for her direction in establishing a helpful research guide with young learners which we can follow. Finally, we are grateful for the advice, support and encouragement of Professor Jo Mynard and the publishing team of Candlin & Mynard ePublishing.

A tribute should be paid to all the classroom and language teachers who actively create an enriching, evolving multilingual world for their students. Community language teachers should be especially acknowledged. Their role in teaching heritage languages continues to make an immense contribution to keeping these languages alive outside the home, invaluable for these students and society, both in the present and for the future.

In Sydney, we marvel at the diversity of languages and people who learn, speak and use these languages. The people and their passion about languages and cultures combine to make Sydney a great metropolis, and we are very grateful that we have the opportunity to present a snapshot from this cultural and linguistic kaleidoscope.

Alice Chik, Susan Markose and Diane Alperstein
Sydney, August 2018

AUTHORS / CONTIBUTORS

Alice Chik

Alice is a Senior Lecturer in Educational Studies and co-ordinator of the Macquarie Multilingualism Research Group. Her research interests include language learning in informal and digital contexts, and multilingualism as urban diversities. Since moving to Sydney in 2014, Alice has taken up strolling in various suburbs to explore and understand languages in the community as a serious hobby. She recently co-edited 'Multilingual Sydney' with Phil Benson and Robyn Moloney (Routledge, 2018).

Susan Markose

For the past fifteen years, Susan has had the pleasure of working as a tutor and occasional lecturer in undergraduate units at the Department of Educational studies, Macquarie University. She has tutored in reading acquisition, educational psychology and intercultural learning. Her published articles report on cross-cultural research findings into family literacy practices and their relation to academic achievement at school. Susan has previously worked as a school teacher at both primary and secondary school levels in Australia and

Diane Alperstein

Di has lived and worked in different multicultural societies from South Africa to Israel, Canada and finally Sydney, Australia, where she has settled and raised her family. She has taught largely in secondary schools and tertiary institutions, with a special interest in the areas of English as a second language, special education, gifted education, and increasingly, multicultural literacy. She enjoys creative writing which constantly reminds her of how difficult language mastery can be. After thirty-five years of teaching, many spent at Macquarie University, she feels it is the intercultural diversity of the students she meets which breathes new life and relevance into every learning experience she has been part of.

Sílvia Melo-Pfeifer

Sílvia Melo-Pfeifer is currently Professor for Foreign Language Education (French and Spanish) at the Department of Education of the University of Hamburg (Germany). She is also a member of CIDTFF (Research Centre "Didactics and Technology in Education of Trainers") at the University of Aveiro (Portugal). Her research interests include: plurilingual and intercultural (on-line) interaction, images of languages, pluralistic approaches to learning and teaching, and heritage language education. She coordinated the educational department at the Portuguese Embassy in Berlin (Germany), between 2010 and 2013. She is currently editing, with Paula Kalaja, the book "Visualising Multilingual Lives: More than Words" (Multilingual Matters).
(silvia.melo-pfeifer@uni-hamburg.de)

Professor Terry Lamb, BSc (Hons), PGCE, MA, PhD, FRSA, Chevalier dans l'Ordre des Palmes Académiques

A former secondary school languages teacher, Terry is Professor of Languages and Interdisciplinary Pedagogy and Director of the Centre for Teaching Innovation at the University of Westminster. He has published extensively in the areas of multilingualism and learner and teacher autonomy and is a founding editor of the academic journal *Innovation in Language Learning and Teaching*. He has carried out consultancies and presented keynote papers in many countries and his numerous research projects have included several at the European Centre for Modern Languages of the Council of Europe in Graz. Terry has worked closely on languages strategy and curriculum with the UK and other Governments and in 2010 was awarded the honour of Chevalier des Palmes Académiques by the French Prime Minister.

Terry is Secretary General (and Past President) of FIPLV (Fédération Internationale des Professeurs de Langues Vivantes), an NGO of both UNESCO and the Council of Europe.

FOREWORD

Terry Lamb

University of Westminster, UK

I have never understood why it is that some people see multilingualism as a problem. Having spent many years as a teacher of French and German in UK secondary [high] schools, struggling to motivate young people to learn another language, it is beyond my comprehension that a child who actually brings their home languages into school is sometimes discouraged from using them. If we value the language learning they do in school, why wouldn't we value the languages they learn outside school? Of course, it isn't always the case that home languages are undervalued or treated with suspicion, but it is more likely to be the case with some languages than with others. My bilingual daughter, whose mother is Austrian, has only ever been met with wonder when people hear her speak German. Rather than suggesting it might be better if she didn't use it or even that she should forget it, in order to avoid causing her confusion as well as creating problems for her English, they have tended to be envious that she has 'simply' grown up bilingually (indeed some have suggested that she was born that way). Yet repeatedly we are confronted by a discourse of negativity about multilingualism, including in the media: schools' poor examination results are considered to be a result of having too many plurilingual students; an improvement in standards is achieved by an amazing new school principal, *despite* most of the children having English as an additional language; the latest civic unrest is brought about by the presence of a range of languages. There was even a senior English politician and member of the cabinet who announced that it would be better for families only to speak English at home rather than their first language in order to avoid problems down the line.

As a young languages teacher in London, I was excited to join a school, in which I could hear a range of languages. Somewhat naïvely, I asked my class of twelve-year-olds to put their hands up if they spoke other languages outside the school. I was completely surprised that no children put up their hands, even though I had heard them speaking other languages outside the classroom, but I put it down to a typical adolescent desire not to stand out from the crowd. However, I did find it rather sad, especially when I realised that some of the monolingual English speakers sometimes teased them for speaking a 'funny language'. This was in the early 1980s, a time when Eric Hawkins was developing his language awareness materials, which my former PGCE tutor had been involved in, so I decided to try out some activities with this class as a way of raising the profile and status of all of the languages spoken by the students. As we used the materials, the class became more and more intrigued by the unusual sounds of different languages, by the different scripts, by the notion that there were families of languages and that the similarities could be detected, and eventually by the fact that others in the class could actually *speak* some of them. Indeed, the children wanted to hear each other's languages in the lessons and to try to imitate the sounds. After a short time, what had been a secret, something unspoken, not mentioned, became a badge of honour; children 'unfortunate' enough not to be able to share stories or sounds of other languages that they spoke outside school began to tell us about distant relatives with girlfriends whose uncle spoke another language – anything to be able to join in with the conversations. Interestingly, it also had an impact on their motivation to learn the French or German I was teaching them – a much greater impact than any of the motivational strategies I had tried out myself.

Ever since then I have argued that multilingualism is of great value not only for those who are plurilingual, who should have the right to use all of the languages that make up their linguistic repertoire, but for everyone. Valuing multilingualism enriches everyone's lives, providing an inroad to valuing people and their family backgrounds, and helping to make connections across cultures (not to mention the other benefits it brings to society, such as the economic ones). For this to happen, however, the diverse languages need to be made audible and visible to *all* in our educational spaces as well as our public spaces (the formal civic spaces of our cities as well as the local neighbourhood spaces) rather than being kept separate in private spaces. In other words, everyone needs to be educated to live and thrive in a multilingual society. Without this the "negative dispositions towards multilingualism are perpetuated across the population, as the value of other languages and, hence, the contribution of the diverse linguistic communities, to the common good remains unarticulated and invisible" (Lamb & Vodicka, 2018).

The collection of illustrations and narratives in this publication produced by Alice Chik, Susan Markose and Di Alperstein makes a valuable contribution to raising the visibility and audibility of our linguistic diversity beyond the individual linguistic communities themselves. Looking through the various body silhouettes with their vast range of languages thoughtfully placed in different areas around their bodies triggered my own somewhat self-indulgent stories at the start of this Foreword. More than any formal research paper or presentation, this publication is able to convey not only the variety of languages that are, quite literally, embodied in the student teachers' contributions, but also the deeply personal and emotional significance that the languages have for these individuals. Reading these explorations of plurilingualism, how could anyone ever again decide that it is a good idea to exclude any of their languages from our classrooms and other public spaces? Clearly language is intertwined with identity, so excluding a language is rejecting part of someone's identity.

These vibrant examples of lived plurilingualism, together with the broad range of reflections and ideas for pedagogical application, provide in themselves a richly valuable resource for teachers not only in New South Wales, but around the world. I have used the body silhouette idea myself in my *Supporting Multilingual Classrooms* workshops (funded by the European Centre for Modern Languages of the Council of Europe) across the length and breadth of Europe, and it resonates with education practitioners working across all sectors, from primary to higher education, from policymaking bodies to teacher education institutions, and including not only languages specialists but those working in a range of disciplines. Recently, in a workshop in Croatia, I introduced it to a group of young volunteers and professionals from across Europe working with refugees and asylum seekers; some of the participants were themselves of refugee background, and they all found the experience illuminating, indeed exciting, and went away with ideas about how they may use the idea themselves, even though the focus of their work was not necessarily on languages. A common reflection, however, was that this was the first time that they had been given the opportunity to share the stories of their own plurilingualism and that they had found the experience not only enlightening, but also emotional, empowering and, in some cases, cathartic. For many, they had never before been aware of how significant their languages were for them and what connotations and memories they triggered. They had taken their languages for granted, partly because they didn't perceive them as interesting or of value to others, but partly because they had never been provided with a tool to enable them to reflect deeply on them. They may have been asked about their languages on occasions, but being asked to consider not only where they belong in their bodies but also why stimulated another level of reflection and engagement.

There is, however, an even deeper significance to this resource than its value as a stimulating and educational tool. Throughout modern history statistics have shown that the 'Australian' teaching body largely consists of white, middle class women. What this collection reveals, however, is that the new teachers in New South Wales who are now joining the workforce are becoming culturally and linguistically much more diverse than in the past. The value of these teachers to their increasingly plurilingual students will be significant, not only because of the languages that they bring with them, but because they will represent a greater diversity of role models for their students and will furthermore, especially after engaging in reflection as demonstrated in this publication, have a much deeper understanding of the significance of their languages for their own identities and growth and, thus, pay much greater attention to their own students' plurilingualism. Such diversity as well as the broad range of personal experiences that comes along with it will be of increasing significance as student demographics continue to change. 53.4% of all government school students in Sydney metropolitan area now have a language background other than English and this is set to increase (NSW Department of Education, 2018). The materials in this publication will provide a heightened visibility, awareness and acknowledgement of the plurilingual knowledge, skills and practices in our classrooms, whilst also enabling teachers to reflect on their own heritage and to draw on it in order to contribute to the shift towards a more open, inclusive valorization of multilingualism.

References

Lamb, T., & Vodicka, G. (2018). Collective autonomy and multilingual spaces in super-diverse urban contexts: Interdisciplinary perspectives. In G. Murray & T. Lamb (Eds.), *Space, place and autonomy in language learning* (pp. 9–28). London, UK: Routledge.

NSW Department of Education. (2018). *Language diversity in NSW 2017*. Accessed on August 15, 2018. https://www.cese.nsw.gov.au//images/stories/PDF/2017_LBOTE_Bulletin_AA.PDF

CHAPTER 1

INTRODUCTION

In today's multicultural classrooms, educators are increasingly entrusted with the education of plurilingual students whose linguistic identities have rarely been foregrounded in classroom interactions (Moloney & Guiles, 2015; Moloney & Saltmarsh, 2016). In order to address the ways of knowing and learning of our diverse student population, it is imperative that educators recognise and incorporate the linguistic and cultural heritage of the students in their classes. To ignore this heritage is to make it more likely that multilingual learners will become monolingual speakers by the time they complete mainstream education in the dominant language (Cummins, 2007). Therefore, an examination of one's systems of beliefs and practices, and the taken-for-granted assumptions of the universality of these beliefs and practices, is an essential prerequisite to critical thinking - of making what is familiar 'anthropologically strange' (Silverman, 2007). This examination begins with a conscious reflection on, and the awareness of, the uniqueness of beliefs and practices as specific to one's own language heritage and learning.

One way to examine beliefs, values and meanings regarding language learning and linguistic identity is for participants to map language experiences to body silhouettes and to record, through narratives, how their attitudes and perceptions are affected by their own language and cultural background. To this end, this action research project required student-teachers, who were undertaking a unit of study on multiculturalism and education, to reflect on what meanings are constructed, the cultural/linguistic influences on these constructions, and how these constructions guided their thoughts, behaviours and worldviews implicit in their linguistic identities (Gadamer, 2004; Wardekkar, 2000). Hence, this action research project worked with students as reflective practitioners to document their experiences with language – both languages that are part of their heritage and those which they undertook as part of their formal learning requirements.

Language portrait silhouettes have been used in previous studies (See for example, Krumm & Jenkins, 2001; Martin, 2012) to document participants' relationships with different languages and how language learning influences learners' beliefs and practices (Chik, 2018). They involve giving participants a blank silhouette of a body on which they colour in the practices, and uses to which they employ the different languages in their repertoire. Colours used are especially indicative of their emotional associations with particular languages (Busch, 2012). As students "unpack the meanings embedded in their self-portraits, we [and they] gain deeper insight[s] into how they individually negotiate their plural identities and internalize language hierarchies within their school and wider society" (Prasad, 2014, p. 68). For teachers, this is an essential step towards developing empathy towards their students, especially linguistic minority students, whose languages and cultures remain invisible in school pedagogies. It also enables student-teachers to acquire an appreciation of the richness in the diversity of worldviews which are inherent in the languages of their students. With such appreciation, it is hoped, will come the resolve to foster the languages of the people of multilingual Sydney.

In Chapter 2, we start with a short introduction to our action research project and data collection method. This section provides a step-by-step guide for teachers and researchers who may want to use language portrait silhouettes for in their classrooms. And this guide is followed by Edward de Bono's Lateral Thinking Skills Program, which is a very straight-forward program to use students' language portraits to further discuss the language learning process, the meanings of languages to individuals, and planning of further learning and resources.

Each language portrait silhouette is accompanied by a short narrative written by the participant (in his/her words). Teachers and researchers can use the drawing and writing as a pair or independently. For instance, language learners can be shown the drawings and have a discussion about the drawings or how languages are presented in the drawing. Alternatively, teachers can show the short narratives and hold a similar discussion. After reading these amazing portraits and narratives, we wrote a short response to each pair of drawing and writing. We also included practical discussion questions for classroom application. Similarly, we would like to emphasize that these questions are only for references, and they can be used with other different portraits as well and in different orders.

In the final chapter (Chapter 3), Sílvia Melo-Pfeifer shares her experiences of using language portraits with young learners in Germany. Her chapter is practical and shows that language portrait is a highly versatile tool for both teaching and researching. Sílvia also provided a step-by-step guide to data analysis. This is a very relevant chapter for teachers planning to analyze the language portraits to inform their teaching, share the findings with other stakeholders (e.g. colleagues and parents), or plan curriculum renewal. For researchers who are new to using visual data, this section provides good references and cautionary tales.

We hope you will enjoy reading the portraits and narratives as mosaic pieces of the multilingual and multicultural tapestry of a metropolitan city. We also wish that you will be inspired to bring these portraits and narratives into your classroom for open discussion about linguistic and cultural diversity, and take the next step to create portraits and narratives. Everyone has a story about language waiting to be told and to be heard, we hope this book is only the beginning of many classroom conversations to come. And if you are interested in conversation about your project or experience, we are just one email away (alice.chik@mq.edu.au)!

References

Busch, B. (2012). The linguistic repertoire revisited. *Applied Linguistics, 33*(5), 502–523.

Chik, A. (2018). Beliefs and practices of foreign language learning: A visual analysis. *Applied Linguistics Reviews, 9*(2/3), 307–332.

Cummins, J. (2007). Rethinking monolingual instructional strategies in multilingual classrooms. *Canadian Journal of Applied Linguistics, 10*(2), 221–240.

Gadamer, H.G. (2004). *Truth and method* (Trans. J. Weinsheimer & D.G. Marshall. 2nd Rev. Ed.). London, UK: Continuum.

Krumm, H.-J. and E.-M. Jenkins. 2001. *Kinder und ihre Sprachen—lebendige Mehrsprachigkeit: Sprachenportraits gesammelt und kommentiert von Hans-Jürgen Krumm*. Eviva.

Martin, B. 2012. Coloured language: Identity perception of children in bilingual programmes. *Language Awareness, 21*(1–2), 33–56.

Moloney, R., & Giles, A. (2015). Plurilingual pre-service teachers in a multicultural society: Insightful, invaluable, invisible. *Australian Review of Applied Linguistics, 38*(3), 123.

Moloney, R., & Saltmarsh, D. (2016). 'Knowing your students' in the culturally and linguistically diverse classroom. *Australian Journal of Teacher Education, 41*(4), 79-93.

Prasad, G. (2014). Portraits of plurilingualism in a French international school in Toronto: Exploring the role of visual methods to access students' representations of their linguistically diverse identities. *The Canadian Journal of Applied Linguistics, 17*(1), 51–77.

Silverman, D. (2007). *A very short, fairly interesting and reasonably cheap book about qualitative research*. Thousand Oaks, CA: Sage Publications.

Wardekker, W. L. (2000). Criteria for the quality of inquiry. *Mind, Culture, and Activity, 7*, 259–272.

CHAPTER 2

THE LANGUAGES, THE PEOPLE, THE PASSION

In this chapter, we will showcase the language portrait silhouettes and complementary stories. We took the following steps to collect these drawings and the written stories:

1. Participants were given the blank silhouette form (Appendix 1);
2. In class, participants discussed the different languages they have learned and/or are learning. They assessed how much they know, comprehend, and/or speak these languages. They shared reflections both through online posts and during tutorial interactions, undertaken during the semester-long course helped our student-teachers develop insights into their own experiences with language and also helped them learn from the experiences of their peers.
3. Then participants discussed what the different languages meant to them.
4. Following from and informed by these contemplations, participants drew and coloured their blank silhouette forms.
5. Participants also wrote a short narrative to explain their drawing and colouring.

This is a simple action research design that can be implemented in classrooms at all levels. It has been used with primary school students in Sydney, Australia (Chik, 2018) and in Hamburg, Germany (Melo-Pfeifer, 2015), with secondary school students in Hong Kong (Chik, 2014) and in Montreal, Canada (Prasad, 2014). Different researchers adapted the research design slightly to cultural differences and classroom needs. So this is a very versatile and simple-to-use research tool.

First, we share stories about languages and people. These stories, drawn by and written in the words of our participant students, document the experiences of young multilingual Australians and record how they are connected emotionally, cerebrally and passionately to various languages. Some extracts are poignant reflections on heritage languages, lost or determinedly nurtured and preserved; some are illustrations of their attitudes to or appreciation of languages learnt in primary and secondary schools; some are linked to languages through popular culture. Whatever the connections, these stories weave a colourful and diverse cultural and linguistic tapestry of Sydney.

Second, we provide a short commentary to each narrative. Our comments are drawn from our repeated reading and analysis of their stories and highlight emerging themes. Frequently, our observations may refer to the content of the written narratives; at other times, they may focus on their visual representations. They are all part of a continuous dialogue on using visual data to better understand language learning and maintenance in Australia.

Third, we integrated Edward de Bono's Lateral Thinking Skills Program for each narrative. We hope that teachers may find the program a helpful way to incorporate and tailor the use of language learning portraits for various teaching and learning purposes. All suggested activities allow for flexibility in adaptation to learners of different languages, ages and learning contexts.

In the next section, we will introduce De Bono's Lateral Thinking Skills Program that can be used as a complementary set of classroom activities. We strongly believe that drawing a language portrait or writing a narrative is only the first step for teachers and learners to explore different aspects of language learning. The Language Portrait Silhouettes offer opportunities to think about the importance of languages in a wider context beyond the classroom. This is clearly acknowledged in the Australian Curriculum's rationale for teaching languages (Australian Curriculum, Assessment and Reporting Authority, 2015).

> *Language learning provides the opportunity for students to engage with the linguistic and cultural diversity of the world and its peoples, to reflect on their understanding of experience in various aspects of social life, and on their own participation and ways of being in the world.*

The statement emphasises the importance of expanding children's thinking in relation to the personal, social, cultural and future career opportunities that "an increasingly interconnected and interdependent world presents". There is a growing awareness in Australia of the value of being bilingual or plurilingual and its diversity in linguistic and cultural resources for social, cultural and economic purposes within local communities and the international world.

The Lateral Thinking Skills Program provides an additional set of tools for teachers to create a space for critical and systematic reflection and discussion of language learning and maintenance. It can be used to

- understand diversity and difference, and be aware of the value of students' own and their classmates' cultural experiences and perspectives;
- develop a deeper understanding of how their culture can influence the world around them, lead to a deeper understanding of themselves, their values, culture and identity;
- explore the purposes of maintaining heritage language and culture as an important means of communication;

- understand that heritage language is defined as more than the language spoken at home; it is all about connections to who you are as a human being, your history and your ancestry; and
- develop stronger intellectual, analytical and reflective capabilities, and encourage creative problem solving and critical thinking.

2.1 Edward de Bono's Lateral Thinking Skills Program: CoRT (Breadth)

Edward de Bono first coined the term 'Lateral Thinking' as an innovative set of thinking skills quite different from traditional problem solving skills which often tries to improve or 'fix' exiting conditions. Instead, thinking itself becomes the commodity which can be directly applied to any situation to generate new ideas and change thinking patterns (de Bono, 1967). Lateral Thinking provides a set of tools which can be used as a deliberate process to produce creative thinking, applying reasoning skills that are not always obvious. This can result in, at times, surprising and unconventional thinking of value to the individual or group. These thinking techniques require systematic and (logical) deliberate practice, which De Bono has likened to the skill of learning to ride a bicycle, the purpose being to reach a 'thinking' destination swiftly and efficiently.

De Bono's Lateral Thinking Program CoRT (Cognitive Research Trust) is useful in the context of language instruction. It provides a teaching framework for examining a student's identity and his or her connection to language and culture; for developing self-esteem and confidence; self-efficacy and metacognitive skills. It is also valuable for teaching generic thinking skills which are transferable to any subject area and to all aspects of life.

The CoRT program provides specific strategies to develop divergent thinking (producing multiple ideas through brainstorming) which can transform thoughts for new purposes and contexts. It encourages students to deliberately select a thinking strategy which will best serve their purpose to solve problems or think creatively in new and exciting ways.

The CoRT program is straightforward and easy to put into practice with whole classes or small groups. The teacher or students may be invited to provide statements or pose problems which relate to authentic issues in the real world. The thinking process (brainstorming and discussion) relating to each strategy should be emphasised without too much time spent on the content (10-20 mins). These strategies are developed in a sequence (1-10) but can be used separately or in clusters. However, it should be noted that they tend to work cumulatively, i.e. earlier thinking strategies will enhance the use of later ones.

Edward de Bono's CoRT Thinking Skills Framework:
1. **PMI** = Plus (Positive), Minus (Negative), Interest (new, innovative ideas).

Deliberate and systematic examination of an idea first for good, then bad and finally interesting points, instead of immediate judgement: acceptance or rejection.

2. **CAF** = Consider ALL factors, notably searching for those you have left out.

Looking as widely as possible at all the factors involved in a situation, instead of only the immediate, most obvious ones.

3. **RULES**

Drawing together the first two lessons. (Optional).

4. **C&S** = Consequence and Sequel (Cause and Effect).

Consideration of the immediate, short, medium and long term consequences, eg. Short term - one year later; medium term - 5 years later; and long term - 10 years later. (The span of time can spread over a far shorter time, or, centuries, depending on the situation and context).

5. **AGO** = Aims, Goals and Objectives.

Picking out and defining objectives. Being clear about one's own aims and understanding those of others; considering the best pathway to achieve one's goals.

6. **PLANNING**

Drawing together the previous two lessons. (Optional).

7. **FIP** = First Important Priorities.

Choosing from a number of different possibilities and alternatives. Prioritising what is essential or works best to solve the problem.

8. **APC** = Alternatives, Possibilities and Choices.

Generating new alternatives and choices, instead of feeling confined to the obvious ones. Seeking out the best possible solution out of those that are available.

9. **DECISIONS**

Drawing together most of the previous lessons. (Optional)

10. **OPV** = Other Points of View.

Moving beyond one's own viewpoint to consider a range of views of others involved in any situation, without judgment or bias.

We have selected topics relating to heritage language and culture in the context of teaching in community language schools. The examples provided under each silhouette can be adapted for different age levels and can be used interchangeably together with other selected strategies. These strategies are especially amenable to group discussions, in language education or regular classrooms.

References

Australian Curriculum Assessment and Reporting Authority (2015). *Languages*. Accessed August 12, 2018 https://www.australiancurriculum.edu.au/f-10-curriculum/languages/

Chik, A. (2014). Constructing German learner identities in online and offline environments. In D. Abendroth-Timmer & E.-M. Hennig (Eds.), *Plurilingualism and multiliteracies: International research on identity construction in language education* (pp. 161–176). Berlin, Germany: Peter Lang.

Chik, A. (2018). Beliefs and practices of foreign language learning: A visual analysis. *Applied Linguistics Reviews*, 9(2/3), 307–332.

de Bono, E. (1967). *The use of lateral thinking*. London, UK: Penguin.

Melo-Pfeifer, S. (2015). Multilingual awareness and heritage language education: Children's multimodal representations of their multilingualism. *Language Awareness*, 24(3). 197–215.

Prasad, G. (2014). Portraits of plurilingualism in a French international school in Toronto: Exploring the role of visual methods to access students' representations of their linguistically diverse identities. *The Canadian Journal of Applied Linguistics*, 17(1), 51–77.

Figure 1. Barbara is a 20-year female student of Aboriginal heritage.

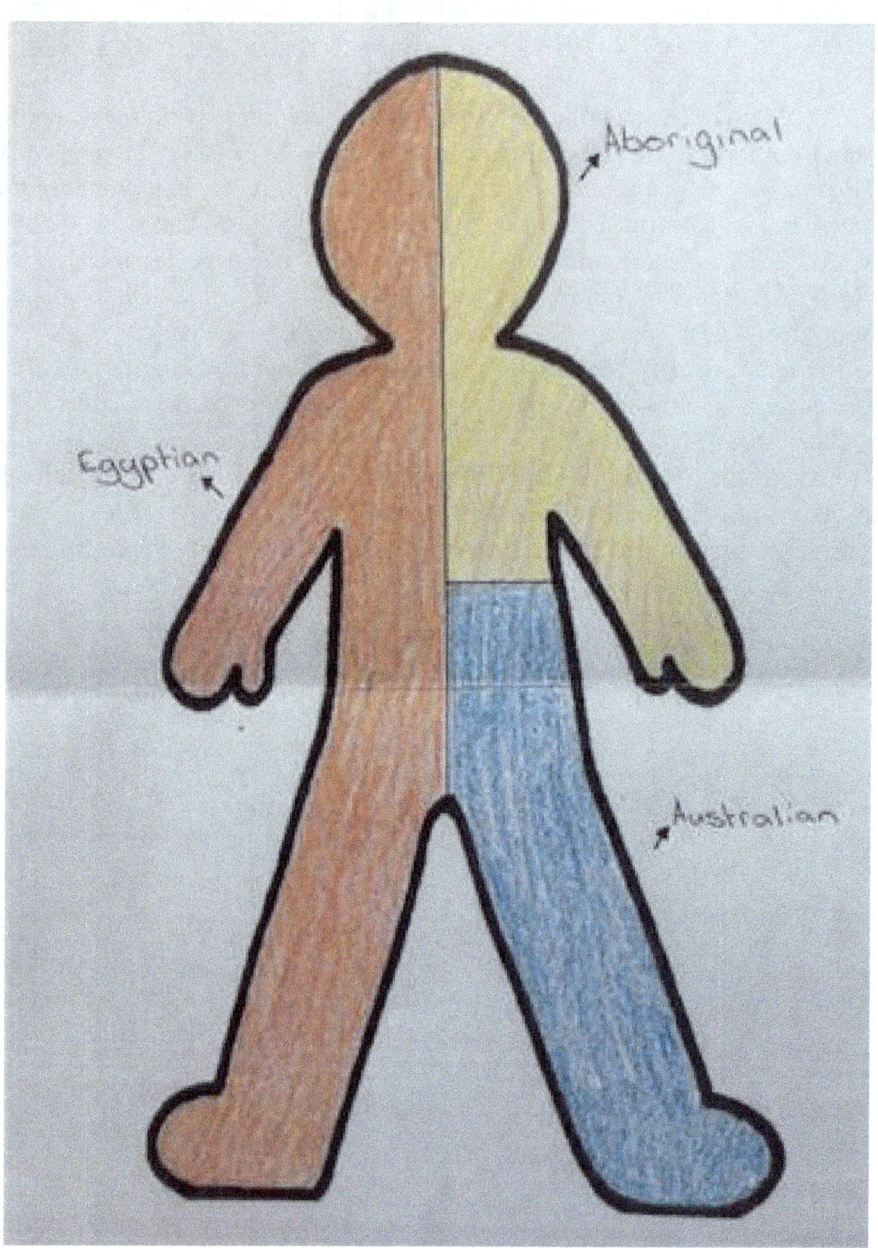

Barbara is a 20-year female student of Aboriginal heritage.

In her words

My silhouette (Fig. 1) is divided into one half and two quarters, this represents the nationalities I am part of. I am half Egyptian, a quarter Aboriginal and a quarter Australian. All of the sections have a distinct divide between them because I feel that none of them mix together. They're all separate parts of me and I find that they only come out at certain times, most of the time I'm Australian because I've got white skin and blue eyes so that's what I appear to be and that's how I'm treated. When I'm with my Mum's side of the family I'm Egyptian there is a deep culture there and majority of the family speaks Arabic (I can't) but I do understand some things. I am also a quarter Aboriginal, that's the part of myself that I know the least about, which is strange because there's just as much Aboriginal blood in me as there is Australian yet somehow I know next to nothing about that part of my heritage. My silhouette represents the what portion of nationalities I am but I feel like the most dominant part would have to be Australian, I'm surrounded by Australian culture and I feel that it has taken over everything.

Our response

It is not unusual to have students of Aboriginal heritage express that they do not know of their Aboriginal languages. Some of these young people are also the first generation to reconnect with their heritage, and thus it is even more important for Aboriginal Languages to have a much stronger presence in every classroom.

Classroom application

Visual – The participant uses a simple division of colours to represent different languages. This can be achieved with crayons and colouring pens. A striking feature of this story is the disconnectedness Barbara experiences as inherent to her various identities. Do some of your students feel the same? Do they see this as problematic? How might they acquire the skills to move seamlessly between their various identities; to blend each identity into a connected whole that is unique to them?

APC – Generating new alternatives and choices, instead of feeling confined to the obvious ones. Seeking out the best possible solution available.

PMI – What are the positive and negative points of not knowing the heritage language from one side of the family?

AGO – If a person decides to learn a new language, how does one proceed? What are some of the considerations?

Keywords: Aboriginal Language, Arabic, language loss, language known, heritage

Figure 2. Tina is a 20-year old female student with home languages in Cantonese and English, and her additional language is Mandarin.

Tina is a 20-year old female student with home languages in Cantonese and English, and her additional language is Mandarin.

In her words

I have shaded the majority of the silhouette in white and yellow, to show my main languages of English and Chinese (Cantonese) as split down the middle (Fig. 2). I have no preference between the two as both are central to my cultural identity. I have included French, Japanese and Korean in the feet because I feel immersed in these languages despite my limited understanding of them. I also chose to position French on the white side as it is a European language and Japanese and Korean on the yellow side. Bright red at the top of the head represents Mandarin which I am currently learning and see as an important, growing aspect of my identity.

Our response

Tina's enthusiasm for learning other languages seems to be related to her choice of the cultures she has most insight into and feels 'comfortable' with (except for French). She is proud to be currently learning Mandarin (coloured bright red) and despite the challenge, this language too is becoming increasingly a part of her identity. Although the portrait suggests a division between her various language identities, her words imply that Tina has been able to incorporate each to be 'central' to her identity. She shows awareness of the relevance of multilingualism in her identity formation and chooses languages accordingly.

Classroom application

Visual – The participant depicts her knowledge of languages through the use colours to represent her linguistic repertoire. This can be done using Microsoft Paint on Windows or a free painting app on a smartphone and a touch-screen tablet.

AGO – Aims, Goals and Objectives. Picking out and defining objectives. Being clear about one's own aims and understanding those of others. Why has the student decided to study all these languages? To what purpose? What are her levels of competence in these? How does she imagine the contribution these languages make in her life?

Keywords: Cantonese, Mandarin, French, Japanese, Korean, identity

Figure 3. Munira is a 20-year old female student with Bosnian as her home language.

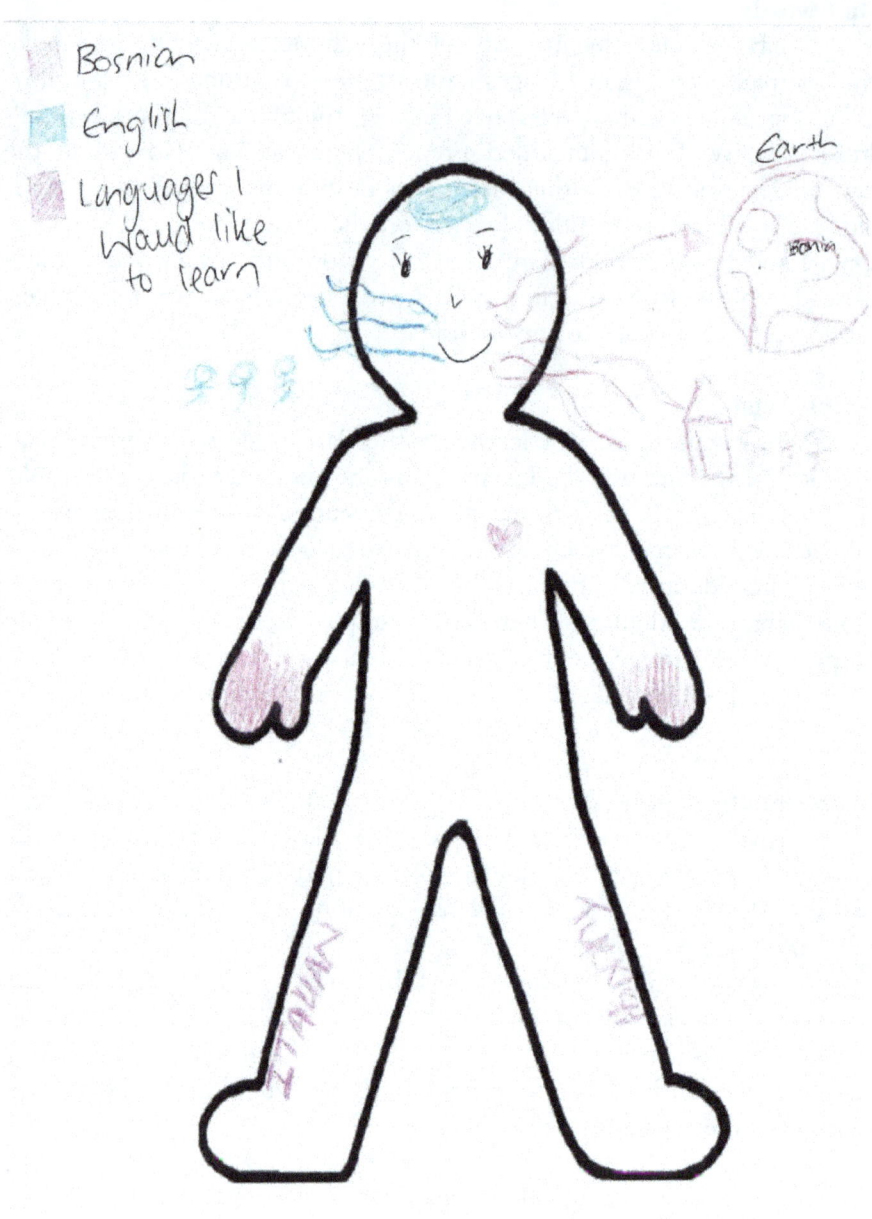

Munira is a 20-year old female student with Bosnian as her home language.

In her words

I chose pink to represent my first language, Bosnian, and blue to represent English, my dominant language (Fig. 3). The pink waves coming from the mouth show that I speak both languages, although blue is darker because it is easier to speak and used more often. The heart is coloured pink, my favourite colour, to symbolise my love for the language I speak at home. Pink waves to the earth connect me to my Bosnian family, while the waves towards the house represent my ability to communicate with my immediate and extended family. The hands are coloured pink because when I speak Bosnian with either family or friends, I tend to "talk with my hands".

Our response

Munira choses her favourite colour, pink, to represent her emotional attachment to her heritage Bosnian language and cultural roots. The waves she draws are linked to symbolic images of the earth, a heart and house which represent the depths of her connection to immediate family, friends and extended family overseas. She enjoys the idea that her Bosnian language affects her personality through her use of expressive hand gestures. While avoiding stereotyping, body language seems to be an area of cultural identity which students could explore further.

Classroom application

Visual – It is very common for younger participants to add expression and emotion to a blank silhouette. However, it is less common to add background objects (e.g. the Earth and the house in this portrait).

AGO – Do you want to set an aim or aims for your language learning? How will you increase your knowledge of the language of your heart? What level of commitment can you set towards the learning of new languages?

FIP – If your learning aim is to communicate with your families and friends overseas, what are your important priorities? Learning to speak and listen? Learning to send an email or text messages?

Keywords: Bosnian, family, gesture

Figure 4. Amy is a 21-year female student with English as her home language. But she continues to learn French and Italian today

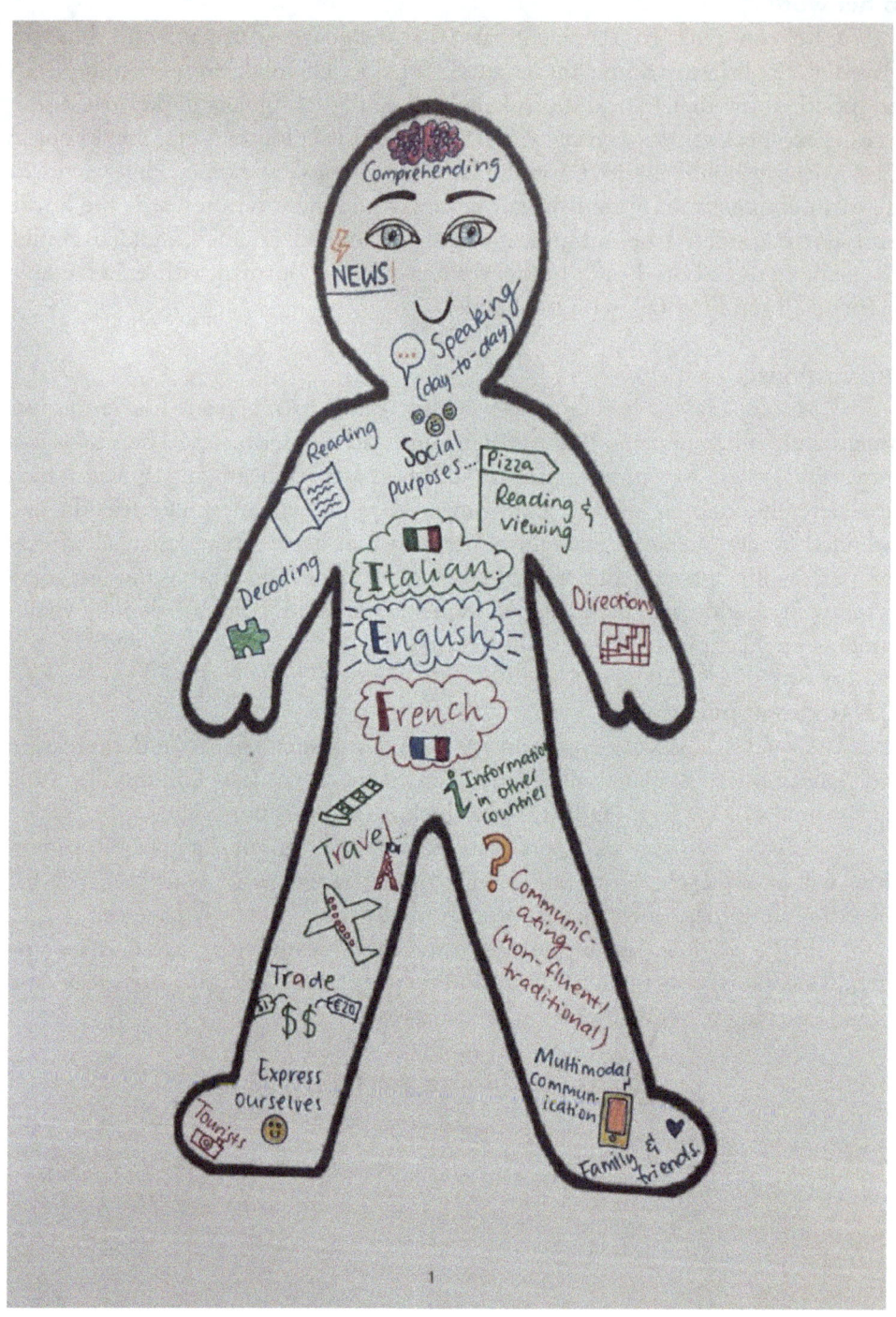

Amy is a 21-year female student with English as her home language. But she continues to learn French and Italian today.

In her words

My connection to each language is shown with one distinct colour (English – blue; French – red; Italian – green) (Fig. 4). I have chosen these colours simply because they represent a key colour on each of the flags where that language is dominant. There is a distinct difference in the way I use each language, which is based upon how I interact with that language. For example, I use English for reading, speaking, decoding and comprehending multimodal forms of communication. Whereas I use French and Italian to read and view, find directions and communicate in a basic manner. These are all depicted through visual and written symbols in my language portrait silhouette.

Our response

Many portraits assigned non-English languages as languages of travel. This phenomenon is more prominent among participants who indicated English as their dominant language and did not mention additional home languages. This could be a topic for discussion with English-dominant students: What are the different languages spoken in Australia? It may be a first step to introducing multilingualism in Australia: languages other than English are not just languages of travel, they are part of languages of Australia.

Classroom application

Visual – This is a more complex construction with a deeper analysis of her language use. It will be a good classroom activity for the participant to talk about her drawing to clarify the concepts.

C&S – If one decides that a language other than English is primarily useful when traveling overseas, what are the consequences for learning?

CAF – What are your opportunities to strengthen your grasp of Italian and French in Australia? Consider all factors, notably searching for those you have left out. Looking as widely as possible at all the factors involved in a situation, instead of only the immediate ones.

Keywords: French, Italian, travel

Figure 5. Atfah is an Urdu and Punjabi heritage speaker, and she first learned English in kindergarten.

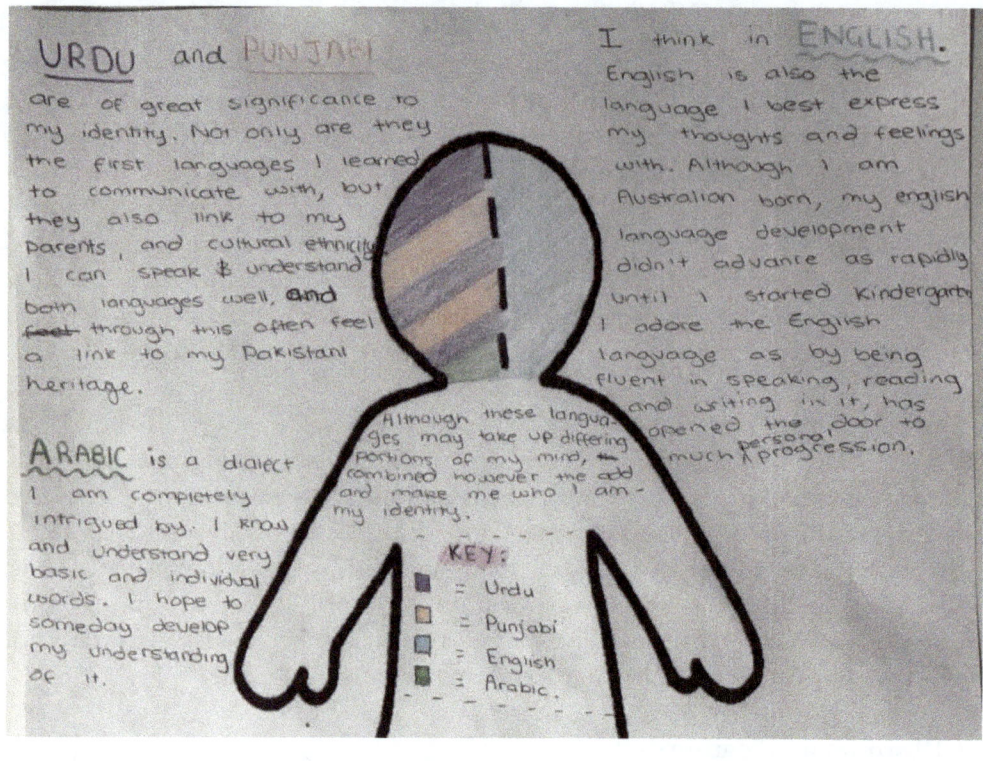

Atfah is an Urdu and Punjabi heritage speaker, and she first learned English in kindergarten.

In her words

Urdu and Punjabi are of great significance to my identity (Fig. 5). Not only are they the first languages I learned to communicate with, but they also link to my parents, and cultural ethnicity. I can speak and understand both languages well, and through this often feel a link to my Pakistani heritage. I am completely intrigued by Arabic. I know and understand very basic Arabic. I think in English, and it is also the language I best express my thoughts and feelings with. Although I am Australian born, my English language development didn't advance as rapidly until I started kindergarten.

Our response

Atfah judges her ability to communicate in her heritage languages of Urdu and Punjabi, and in the language of her birth country - English, to be competent. She emphasises in her silhouette that it is the combination of all three (along with a small portion of Arabic) that "...make up who I am". Competency in her heritage languages together with confidence in English are very positive factors in her larger cultural identity.

Classroom application

Visual – Some participants tend to put in a lot of writing immediately next to their colouring and drawing. This can be very helpful for teachers in their interpretation of their students' thoughts. Words in their writings may also be used as prompts to further discussion in class.

OPV – Many participants wrote about heritage languages and cultures as belonging to their parents and grandparents. Do your students feel the same way? What value does the cultivation of heritage language competencies have for each child in the class?

OPV – How do you feel about others who are more immersed in their cultures and prefer to use their heritage languages when they are together in social groups?

Keywords: Urdu, Punjabi, Arabic, family, heritage

Figure 6. Zebadiyah is a 21-year old male student who speaks English and Malay at home, and he learnt Arabic.

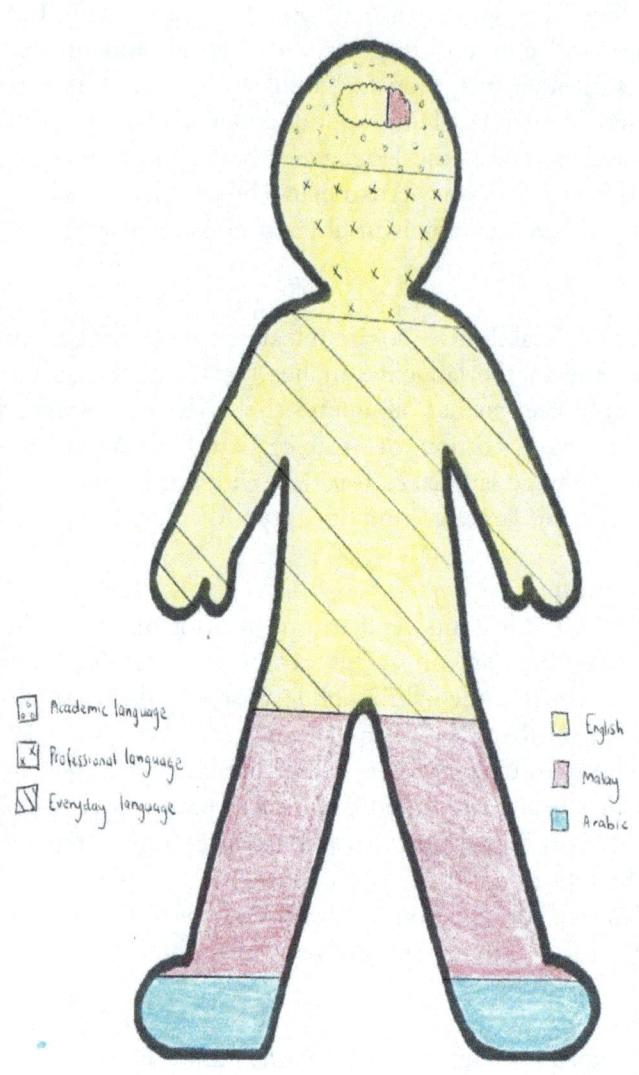

Zebadiyah is a 21-year old male student who speaks English and Malay at home, and he learned Arabic and Italian.

In his words

I have coloured my silhouette to represent my exposure to, and use of many languages throughout my life (Fig. 6). My exposure to English has come from schooling and living in an Australian society. The red represents my exposure and use of Malay, which is quite prominent but not used as often as English. My exposure to Malay comes from my parents and their Singaporean Malay backgrounds, while my use of Malay is used for communicating with them at home. My exposure to Arabic came from my Muslim upbringing, while my use of it is solely for religious purposes (prayer and recitations).

Our response

When it comes to the languages used for communication and expression, Zebadiyah has demarcated his professional and academic self from his everyday self. While English is the language used in an academic context and during his interactions with the wider Australian society, Malay is the language of the home, and remains quite 'prominent' in his communicative repertoire. He sees languages as serving many different purposes in his life, academic, professional, social and religious, rather than in terms of identity.

Classroom application

C&S – Some participants mentioned using their heritage languages in some specific contexts (e.g. only with their families, or for religious purposes). What are the consequences of limiting a language to some contexts and some people?

APC – Alternatives, Possibilities and Choices. Can Malay or Arabic be developed to enable access to literature in those languages?

Keywords: Malay, Arabic, identity, Muslim

Figure 7. Zinovia is a 20-year old female student who speaks Greek and English at home, and learned some German.

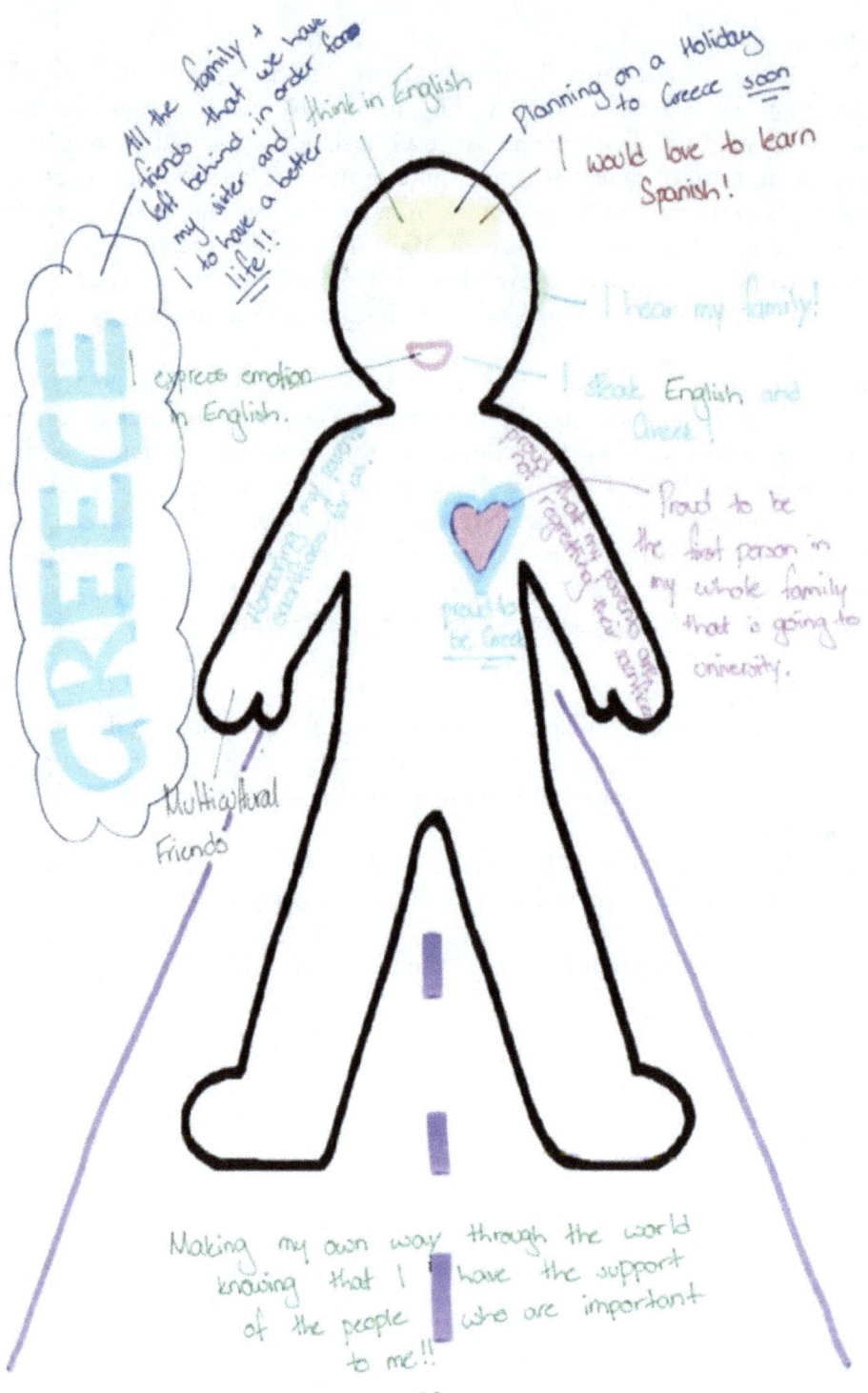

Zinovia is a 20-year old female student who speaks Greek and English at home, and learned some German.

In her words

My silhouette is divided into three sections (Fig. 7). The head shows all my thoughts and the way I express myself. From the top of the shoulders to the end of the arms show all my feelings about my parents' sacrifices and my own achievements; and the legs signify my future path. The use of multiple colours represents significant points. Blue symbolises everything important and influential, such as my background, culture and family left behind in Greece. A pink heart represents all my feelings; green represents the importance of English in my life; and finally, red indicates my desire to learn Spanish. I am standing on the road making my way through the world, supported by all those who are important to me.

Our response

Zinovia has a strong emotional attachment to her Greek culture and roots. She refers to her 'parents' sacrifices', separation from family left behind, as well as pride in her own achievements, being the first of her Greek family to attend university. Although she expresses emotions in English, she can speak Greek and her attachment to her Greek heritage largely influences her life and the choices she makes.

Classroom application

Visual – It is not very common for a participant to draw a background. In this case, the drawing of a road seems to give additional motion to the portrait!

CAF – Consider all factors. When students express an emotional link to a language, can this link be the motivation required to learn the language? The class may like to discuss what processes and technologies may be tapped to help the child use his/her speaking and listening competencies in a language to develop writing and reading skills in that language? Is there a partner in class who can accompany the child in this journey?

Keywords: Greek, emotion, family

Figure 8. Mark is a 22-year old male student who speaks English at home, but learned Korean.

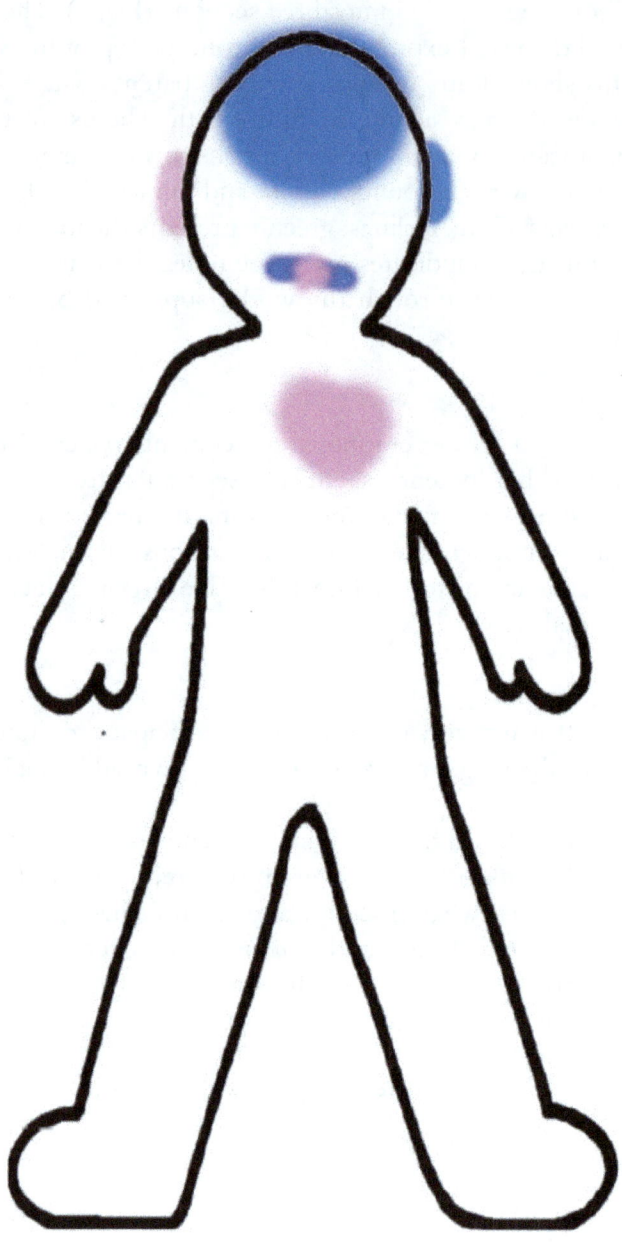

Mark is a 22-year old male student who speaks English at home, but learned Korean.

In his words

I speak English and Korean (Fig. 8). I have only learnt Korean as an adult over the last four years and have had a great time visiting Korea earlier in the year as an exchange student. Pink represents the Korean language to me, the pink cherry blossoms being one of my favourite memories of Korea. The pink heart represents my desire to become fluent in Korean, as well as the emotional reaction I have when hearing the language, such as watching Korean movies. English is a more academic language for me, but I always make an effort to speak both English and Korean in my day to day life.

Our response

Mark is not of Korean heritage. He taught himself the language as an adult and has developed an intense emotional connection to it. Learning Korean has been a labour of love for him '[It] has taken up every corner of my free time over the last four years'. He has been on student exchange to Korea and has also actively sought friends with whom he can further develop his language skills. His romantic attitude seems evident in his favourite memory of pink cherry blossoms in bloom in the Korean springtime. Learning a new language can have an unexpected emotional and motivating effect on an individual, as evident in Mark's personal experience.

Classroom application

APC – A study abroad trip may be a very good reason to start the language learning process. What about when the learners are back home? What are some alternative or possible language learning opportunities we can create inside and beyond the classroom? For Mark, the company of Korean speakers was a resource he could tap. Can you create such a circle of friends?

Keywords: Korean, travel, self-study

Figure 9. Olivia is a 20-year old female student who speaks Kirundi and English at home, and learned French and Swahili.

Olivia is a 20-year old female student who speaks Kirundi and English at home, and learned French and Swahili.

In her words

I was born in Tanzania and lived there for 8 years (Fig. 9). I learnt to speak Kirundi and Swahili. I don't speak Swahili as much because I don't come in contact with a lot of people who speak the language which resulted in forgetting the language to some extent. But I don't feel like it has had a negative impact because I can still understand and respond to some words in Swahili. Kirundi (orange) is a big part of my life, the language which is spoken at home, but English (yellow) is my strongest form of communication. Both Kirundi and Swahili are brightly coloured, but red highlights how Swahili is in 'danger' of becoming lost because I am not able to write and read in Swahili, placed at the foot of the drawing as my ability to understand it decreases dramatically.

Our response

Olivia's loss of some of her second heritage language is due to lack of practice with social groups speaking Swahili, and her inability to read or write it. Her first language, Kirundi, which is spoken at home most of the time, remains a "big part of [her] life". Her fluency in Kirundi is offset by some concern about the increasing loss of the second one, which she sees as, "in danger" of being lost" and "decreasing rapidly". Children may have an attachment to more than one heritage language which they regard as an important connection to their roots.

Classroom application

APC – The lack of access to a speech community is a challenge for language learners. However, this challenge can increasingly be overcome with online social media tools and language exchange platforms/apps. Can you locate an online language exchange group?

Keywords: Kirundi, French, Swahili, language loss

Figure 10. Zeel is a 20-year old female student who speaks English and Hindi at home.

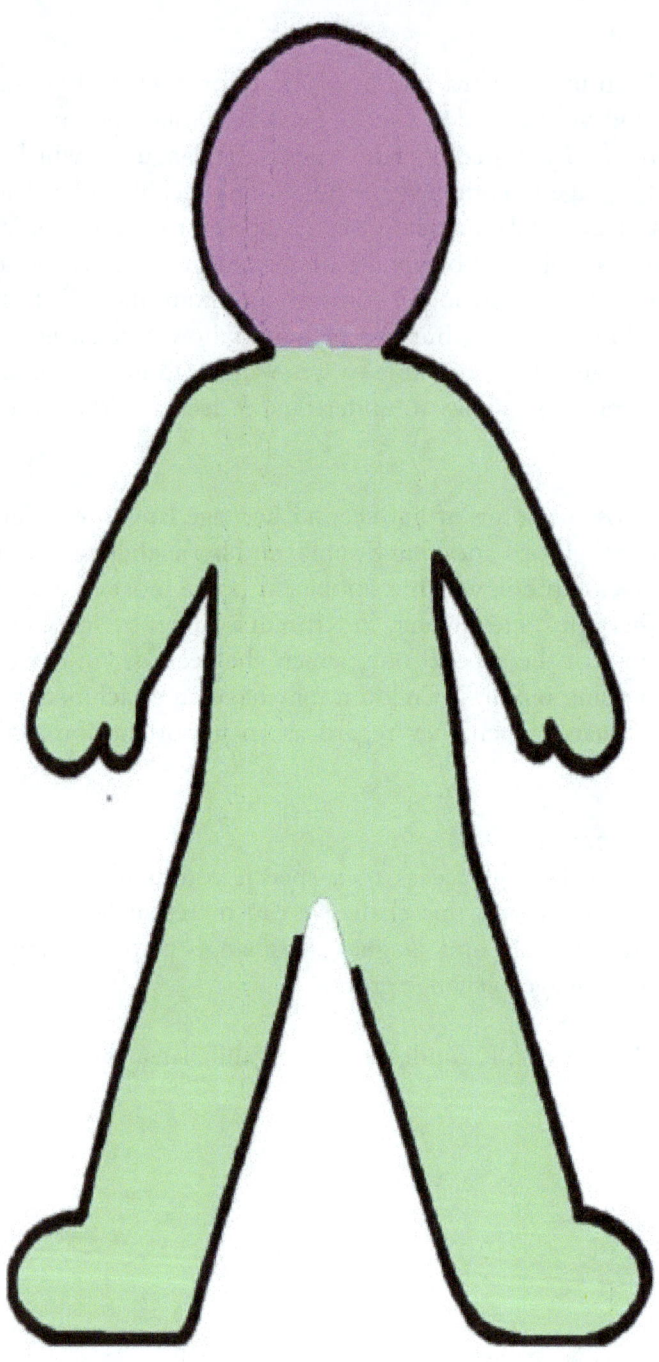

Zeel is a 20-year old female student who speaks English and Hindi at home.

In her words

I make a concerted effort, and struggle at times, to translate English into Hindi, but my parents encourage me to retain my Hindi language skills for the purpose of communicating with my grandparents when I travel overseas (Fig. 10). My strong emotional connection to my grandfather's memory is represented in purple, his favourite colour. It also symbolises my spiritual connection to Hindi and desire to expand my knowledge of the language. English is, however, a big part of my life, symbolised by green which 'calms' and 'rejuvenates' me.

Our response

For Zeel, it isn't always easy to switch from English to Hindi; it is a 'struggle' but she is impelled to retain her Hindi language skills. Hindi is her link to her heritage, her history and her family.

Classroom application

C&S – Some participants mentioned using their heritage languages in some specific contexts (e.g. only with their families, or for religious purposes). What are the consequences of limiting a language to some contexts and some people? Can we expand when and where we may use our heritage languages? How might we improve our skills with the language so we have sufficiently strong skills in order to pass on our heritage to the next generation?

Keywords: Hindi, family, grandparents, heritage

Figure 11. Sofia is a 19-year old female student who speaks English and Spanish at home.

Sofia is a 19-year old female student who speaks English and Spanish at home.

In her words

My silhouette is a blend of colours representing English, Spanish and German (Fig. 11). My heritage language is German. Although I learned it when I was younger, I have completely lost it. I regret the disconnection with my German heritage and have filled the void by learning Spanish, the language of my Argentinian stepmother. I believe in the value of another language and symbolise this with a heart because language means so much to me, I find it priceless.

Our response

Sofia clearly indicates her regret for her disconnection with her German heritage. She has compensated for this to some extent, by learning Spanish, which 'surrounded' her as a child at home. She indicates that she was pleased to fill this void, as she values knowing another language. It can also be interpreted that the loss of heritage language is perceived with the sadness of loss of identity.

Classroom application

Visual – Many participants like to write directly next to their portraits, and this can be quite handy if the teacher does not have the time to go through everything during the same lesson.

C&S – It is very interesting that the participant substitutes one language for another, and both languages connect with families. In this case, will the learning of Spanish help the learner to 'regain' German?

CAF – Since there is an entire extended family who speaks German, can SE regain the language of her childhood through interactions with her family? How many hours of conversational practise would be required to develop her language skills in German and Spanish? How many family members would she need to speak to each week? What else must she do to develop these skills?

Keywords: German, Spanish, family, emotion, language loss

Figure 12. Janice is 21-year old female student who speaks Vietnamese and English at home, and learned Japanese later.

Janice is 21-year old female student who speaks Vietnamese and English at home, and learned Japanese later.

In her words

I am fluent in speaking Vietnamese, my heritage language, but would like to continue increasing my written skills and vocabulary (Fig. 12). I am aware that I am mixing English and Vietnamese all the time and it is this combination of languages that makes up my identity. When I was younger I did not really appreciate how my parents made me go to a Vietnamese school every week. However, it benefits me a lot because I can speak and write in Vietnamese and understand more difficult conversations (e.g. metaphors…etc.).

Our response

Janice is comfortable code-switching between English and Vietnamese. While acknowledging this, she does not view her mannerism in a negative light. Looking back, she acknowledges the importance of attending Vietnamese community school, as she not only speaks and writes Vietnamese, but can understand it at a more complex level.

Classroom application

AGO - Do you hope to improve your writing skills and vocabulary in the language you are learning? Define your short-term and long-term aims, goals and objectives to achieve your desires. What are your parents' aims, goals and objectives for you in relation to your language classes? How might you work towards a common purpose, a common objective?

Keywords: Vietnamese, Japanese, family, code-mixing

Figure 13. Ella is a 22-year old female student who speaks English at home but learned French in school.

Ella is a 22-year old female student who speaks English at home but learned French in school.

In her words:

I chose to represent English (my first language) in blue, while French (a secondary language I learnt in high school) in green (Fig. 13). I have grown up in a household that speaks only English. My father comes from an English background and my mother is half Indian, however the language was not passed on through her side of the family. In high School, I learned French for five years, but decided not to continue with it for my High School Certificate (HSC). This is reflected in my drawing in green as there are still some French words and phrases I remember, however, most of the language is 'evaporating' because I no longer use it.

Our response:

This is a story of opportunity lost. There are many speakers who have not had the opportunity to learn their heritage language. This could be for very complex reasons. Perhaps we can also look in why students would give up learning a language after five years.

Classroom application

PMI (and OPV)- What might be the pluses, minuses and interesting aspects of reconnecting with a parent's language, when it was lost to your parent?

OPV - What does the rest of the class think about this issue?

CAF - How might we relearn and maintain a language so it is not lost to us?

Keywords: French, language loss, heritage

Figure 14. Lily is a 21-year old female student who speaks English and Maltese at home, and learned Italian.

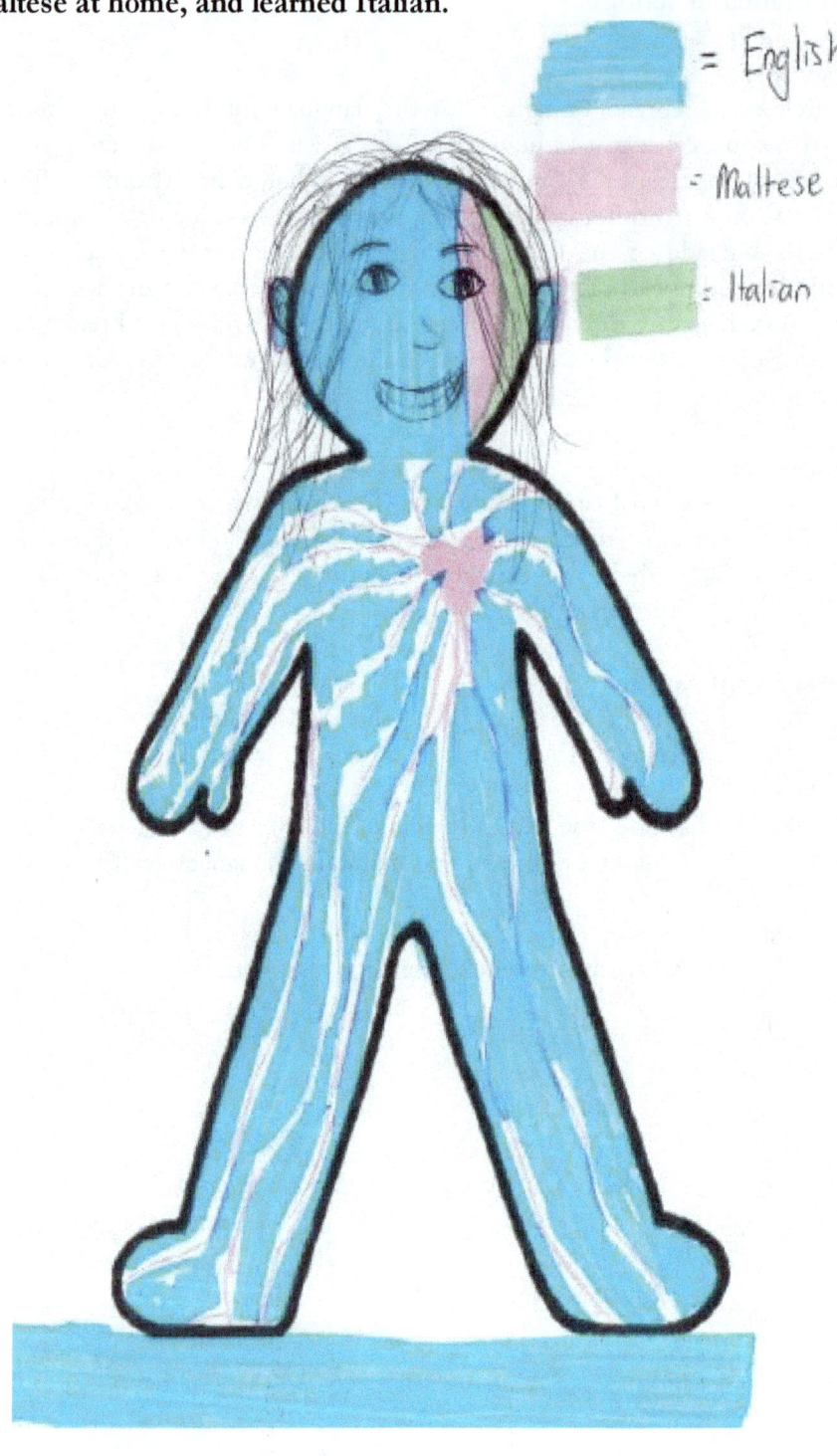

Lily is a 21-year old female student who speaks English and Maltese at home, and learned Italian.

In her words:
Both my parents and I were born in Australia and therefore grew up in a country that is predominantly English (blue). All my grandparents were born in Malta and therefore speak fluent Maltese, and I therefore coloured some of the ears in pink to represent that I do hear this language (Fig. 14). Maltese also is a language I hold very dear to me as it is so important to my family. Therefore, while majority of the silhouette is coloured blue, pink is flowing throughout, starting from the heart to represent this connection. Finally, I learnt Italian from Year 8 to 10 in high school, and therefore am able to understand and speak a tiny bit of Italian.

Our response:
Lily continues her links with Maltese, the language of her grandparents. She speaks it at home and hears it in her environment. There is a lot of discussion about children losing interest in language learning, but sometime people also come back and revisit their language in later years.

Classroom application
FIP – Do you want to learn the language of your grandparents? Do you want to progress in the language you learnt at school? What are your priorities?

Keywords: Maltese, Italian, family, grandparents

Figure 15. Raaina is a 22-year old female student who speaks English and Arabic at home.

Raaina is a 22-year old female student who speaks English and Arabic at home.

In her words:

I divide my silhouette into four components, using colours and body parts to symbolise their significance (Fig. 15). My heritage language is Arabic, but I regard this as my second language, English being my first (grey, mouth). My parents speak Arabic, but I am not entirely fluent in speaking it myself. I have a strong desire to read, write and speak Arabic more fluently and struggle at times with writing, lacking deeper knowledge of grammatical rules (symbolised by the green brain and ears). The heart symbolises my emotional connection to this heritage language, including my link to my religion. "It defines me as an individual" (blue, heart).

Our response:

Raaina predicament lies in a lack of foundation in language skills such as grammar and punctuation. She yearns to master these skills which would provide her with confidence in reading, writing, comprehending and speaking the language. The Arabic language, depicted by a heart, is a central component of her identity and religious affiliation.

Classroom application

FIP – What are your priorities? If fluency in speech and listening comprehension are your priorities, what resources can you tap to develop these abilities? If formal language skills of grammar and written expression are important, how will you learn these? Can you see an advantage for developing both sets of skills at the same time?

Keywords: Arabic, emotion, heritage, family

Figure 16. Deanne is a 33-year old female student who speaks English at home, and learned Spanish and French.

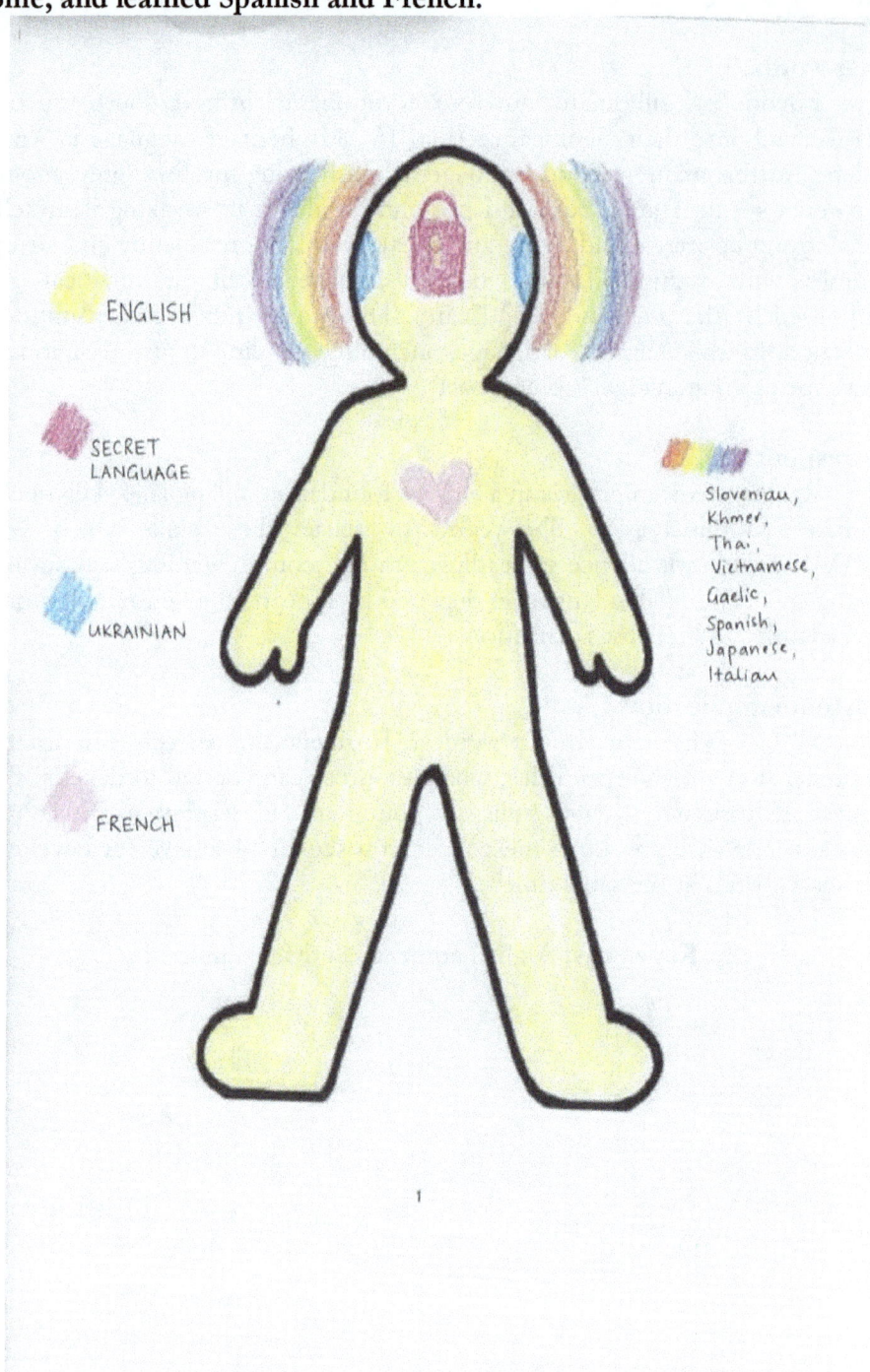

Deanne is a 33-year old female student who speaks English at home, and learned Spanish and French.

In her words

The only language I am fluent in is English (yellow) (Fig. 16). I have always loved French and hope to learn it one day – this language is so feminine and pretty (a pink heart). My sister and I and two of our friends created a secret language when we were young, it has been stored inside my brain for over 20 years (the fun colour purple in the shape of a lock). The blue near my ears is Ukrainian – I heard this language quite a bit when I was younger from my Ukrainian paternal grandparents, but I never learned the language myself so it stayed in my ears only. Outside of those languages most close to me, I have been exposed to a range of other languages either through high school (Spanish), languages my sister learned in school (Japanese), my maternal Irish family (Gaelic), my boyfriend's family (Slovenian and Italian) or through countries I have travelled to (Khmer, Thai, Vietnamese). I know a few basic words in these languages. I think of these as a rainbow of languages, close to my ears and brain, but not part of me.

Our response

Sometime languages come to us from many different directions. It is interesting that the speaker is exposed to a number of languages other than French, yet French is the only language she said she wanted to learn. What is her attachment to French? Or is it because of the social representation of the language ('feminine and pretty')?

Classroom application

FIP – What are your priorities? How can you turn a desire for language acquisition to action and then to competencies in that language? When you hear language in practice all about you, what value do these languages hold for you?

Keywords: Spanish, French, Ukrainian, Japanese, Gaelic, Slovenian, Italian, Khmer, Thai, Vietnamese, travel, family

Figure 17. Dustan is a 24-year old male student who speaks German at home.

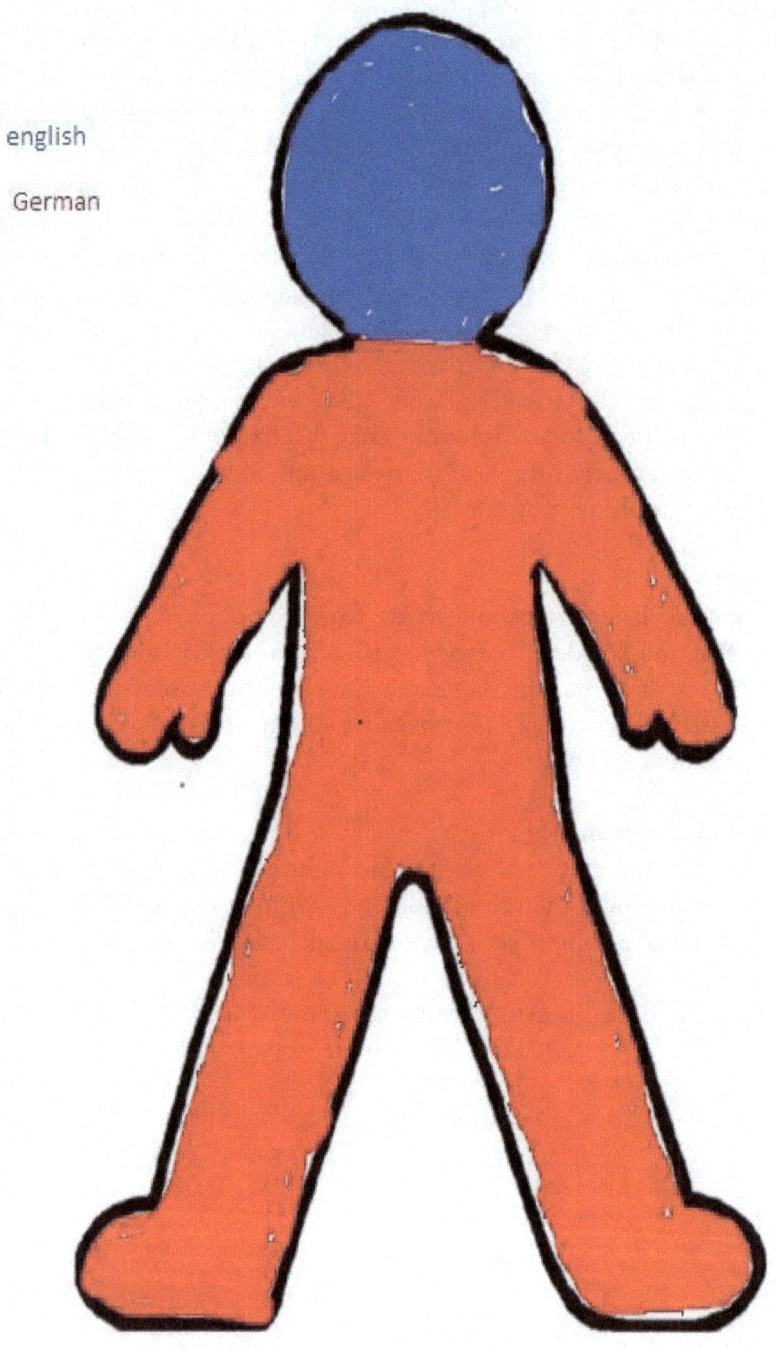

Dustan is a 24-year old male student who speaks German at home.

In his words

I grew up speaking German at home, although I learnt English as well (Fig. 17). Living in Australia has favoured my English skills and this relative capacity for each language is shown in my silhouette. German, centred in the brain, requires more cognitive effort than English, perhaps due to less practice.

Our response

Dustan identifies German as more cognitively challenging than English although he spoke this language at home. Perhaps, heritage language, when spoken only in certain contexts (typically the home), can become isolated and not practised in the individual's wider social life. This will then contribute to language loss.

Classroom application

Visual – This style can be easily done with a Microsoft Paint or other painting apps on a tablet.

CAF – Can the language of the home be strengthened even when all members of the immediate and extended family speak English? How can the heritage language be strengthened? What level of commitment is needed to do so? Can certain hours of a day be devoted only to speaking that language

Keywords: German, challenge

Figure 18. Pareesa is a 21-year old female student who speaks English and Arabic at home, and learnt Italian.

Pareesa is a 21-year old female student who speaks English and Arabic at home, and learnt Italian.

In her words

My language portrait is divided up in two colours: purple for Arabic and blue for English (Fig. 18). Purple and blue are my favourite colours and being able to speak fluently in two languages is something of great importance to me. The wavy line used to separate the two colours within the figure is indicative of how intermingled these languages are with each other and how I communicate. The wavy lines streaming from the figures are mixed in both purple and blue. Both languages are used externally to communicate. When I speak to my parents, I would say some words in Arabic and then continue with English and vice versa. As my family speak more English, I speak Arabic less. If you had asked me to colour in this figure in a few years, you would find more blue and less purple.

Our response

Pareesa emphasises the value she places on her ability to speak both English and Arabic fluently. She code-switches between the two with ease to communicate with her parents. At the same time, she indicates in her silhouette that English (blue shading) has prominence over Arabic (purple shading). Arabic is gradually being used less and less as parents master English. She imagines this pattern continuing into the future. It appears inevitable that her language choices will see her gravitating to the dominant language to the detriment of her heritage language.

Classroom application

Visual – It is quite unusual for a participant to include external influences on her language learning. By using the two different colours, the participant brilliantly presented her code-mixing of English and Arabic.

CAF – What helps your parents learn a language? How important is practice in language learning? What is most important for you about your heritage language? List these. How will you feel if your skill in the language deteriorates? What can you do about it?

Keywords: Arabic, code-mixing

Figure 19. Jack is a 21-year old male student who speaks English and Italian at home, and learned French, Korean, Mandarin, and Japanese.

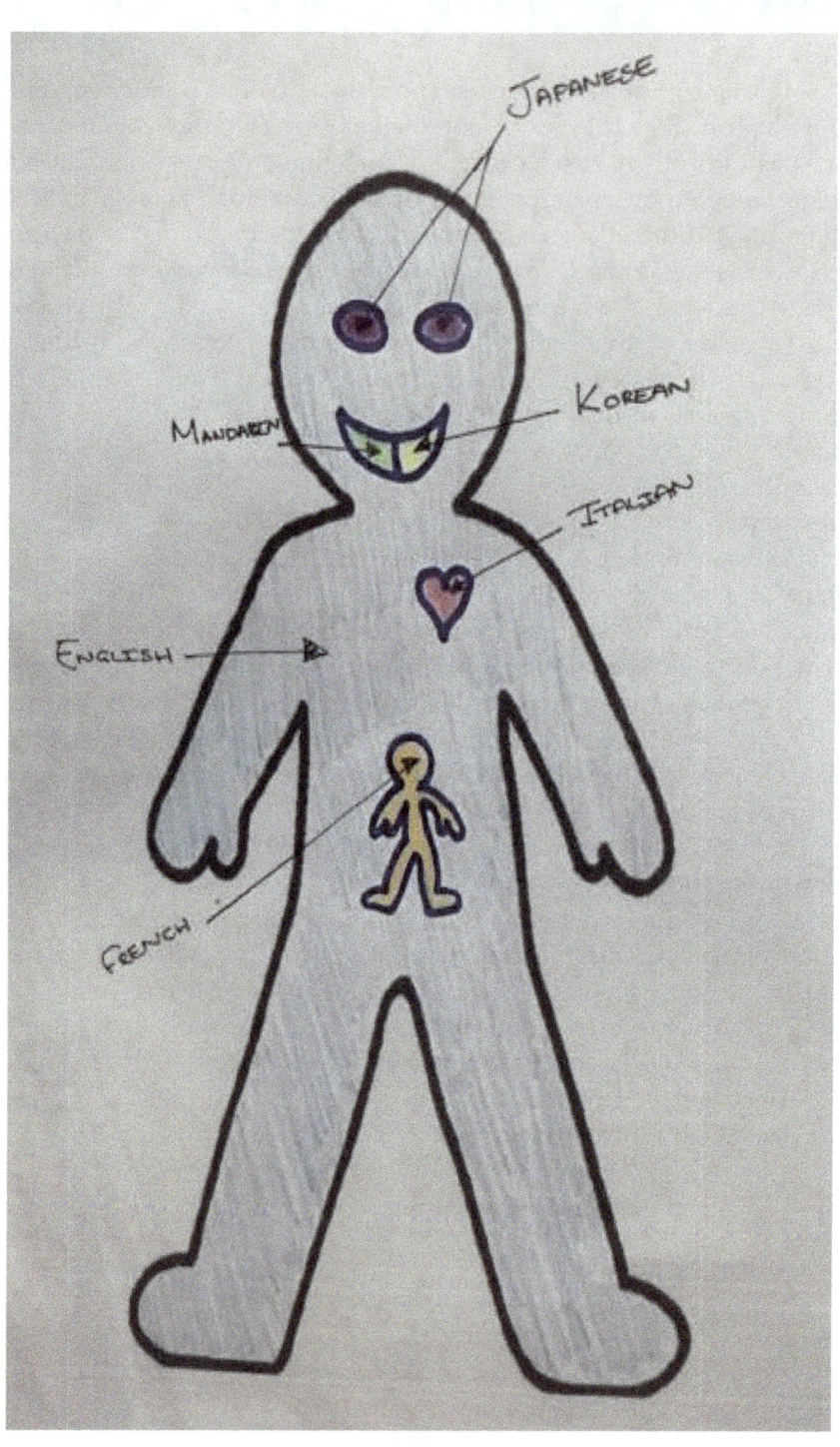

Jack is a 21-year old male student who speaks English and Italian at home, and learned French, Korean, Mandarin, and Japanese.

In his words

English is my only confidently spoken language, but I love Italian, my heritage language (coloured in a red heart), which my grandparents and mother speak fluently (Fig. 19). I feel a connection to several other languages which provide an overall view of who I am and the way certain languages combine to make up my identity. An image of a smaller person inside myself represents my connection to French, which I learnt from K-6 in Primary School, although retaining very little of it. Japanese makes up "my eyes" and being able to identify phrases from many hours watching Anime on TV. Mandarin and Korean, through my mouth connect me to my friends at school.

Our response

Although his love for his heritage language, Italian, is depicted by his Italian heart, Jack is connected to several other languages acquired in different spaces: French, learnt early at school, Mandarin and Korean, through school friends, and Japanese by viewing Anime on TV. Jake has accessed several languages through a diversity of mediums, both formally and informally, without necessarily learning these in any depth. He views languages from a wider perspective, recognising how these contribute to his identity.

Classroom application

Visual – This is an unusual portrait because includes 'a little person', and that little person indicates the participant's identity.

FIP – What are your language priorities for Italian and the other languages you know? How can your heritage language be of value to you later? List these. What skills would you like to acquire? What investment, in terms of time and resources would you need to make so can you acquire these?

Keywords: Italian, French, Japanese, Mandarin, Korean, pop culture, friends, travel, identity

Figure 20. Jayden is a 22-year old male student who speaks Korean and English at home, and learned French.

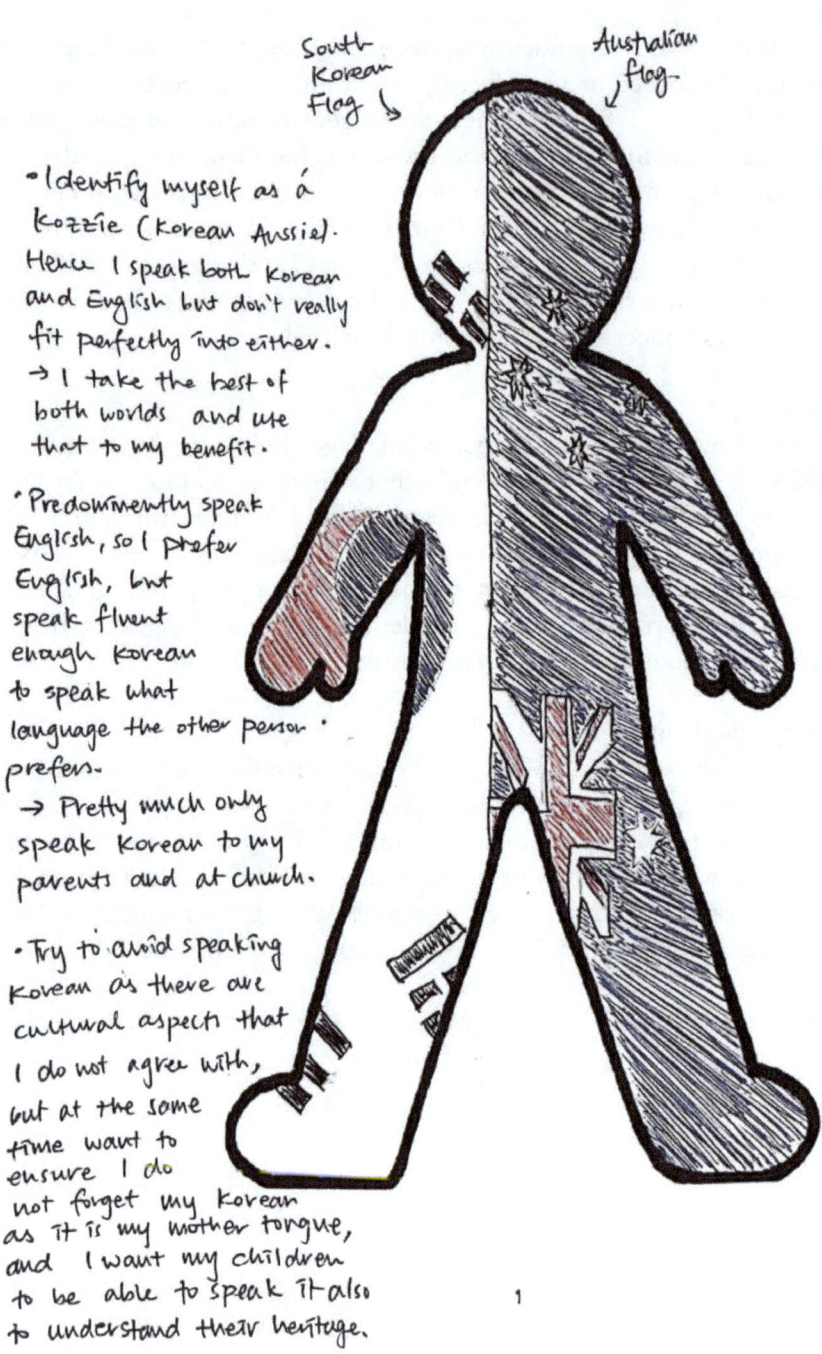

Jayden is a 22-year old male student who speaks Korean and English at home, and learned French.

In his words

The two main languages I speak are English and Korean, that is why the two flags are drawn (Fig. 20). However, I prefer English (although Korean was my first language) so the Australian flag takes up more space than the Korean flag. I speak fluent enough Korean to read, write, speak, and understand it. Although I prefer English, between the two languages, I speak whichever language the other person prefers.

Our response

Jayden appears to be confident in speaking his heritage language, although he favours English. He shows this ease and flexibility in transitions between language, largely influenced by his interactions with others and the language they choose to speak in. He also identifies as 'Kozzie' (Korean Aussie) to 'take the best of both worlds and use that to my benefit'. This may be a very pragmatic approach to heritage language maintenance and yet he confesses that he tries to 'avoid speaking in Korean' as there are cultural aspects he does not 'agree with'.

Classroom application

Visual – It is quite common for participants to include national flags in their portraits. To some extent, we still have a strong concept that a language is associated with only one country, but there are many languages that have a strong global presence (e.g. Spanish, Arabic, and Chinese and indeed Korean).

CAF – What is your identity? Is it important to choose one or the other identity? Is there a defined way of 'being' that is specific to one identity? Can you pick and choose how you might want to express that identity? Or do you believe that cultural identity cannot change? What would you do if you did not like some aspect of your culture?

Keywords: Korean, identity, church

Figure 21. Saiqa is a 20-year old female student who speaks English and Arabic at home, and learned French in school.

Saiqa is a 20-year old female student who speaks English and Arabic at home, and learned French in school.

In her words

The green in the brain area is to show that I think in Western ways (Fig. 21). I think in English and am not heavily set on traditional Lebanese ways of thinking. The speech bubble attached shows that I still pertain to Arab customs. The ears are in both green and blue to show that I understand both languages. The lips and hands are green to show that English is my first language. The heart is green because English as a language is a comfort for me that I can rely on. Specks of blue show that I can speak a little Arabic. The speck of blue in the heart is the connection I have with family that only speak Arabic such as my grandparents and a few aunts/uncles overseas. The specks of blue throughout show that Arabic has always been there in the background, but hasn't been a major influence on my life or way of thinking.

Our response

Saiqa makes a clear distinction between thinking in "western ways' while retaining some traditional cultural Arab customs. She speaks little Arabic. English in the other hand is a 'comfort' to her, something she can 'rely on'. Her words may reflect the insecurity which second language users feel when they are caught between their heritage and dominant country cultures and languages.

Classroom application

Visual – Many participants allocated and differentiated languages to brain or heart. The brain is frequently 'occupied' by the dominant language (and usually not the heritage language), but the heart is 'filled' with a heritage language. In this case, both English and Arabic have a place in her heart.

C&S – What are the consequences of maintaining your heritage language? What are the consequences of losing your heritage language? If you were to advise someone about maintaining their heritage language, what would you say?

Keywords: Arabic, identity

Figure 22. Aayah is a 22-year old female student who speaks English and Urdu at home, and learned French at school

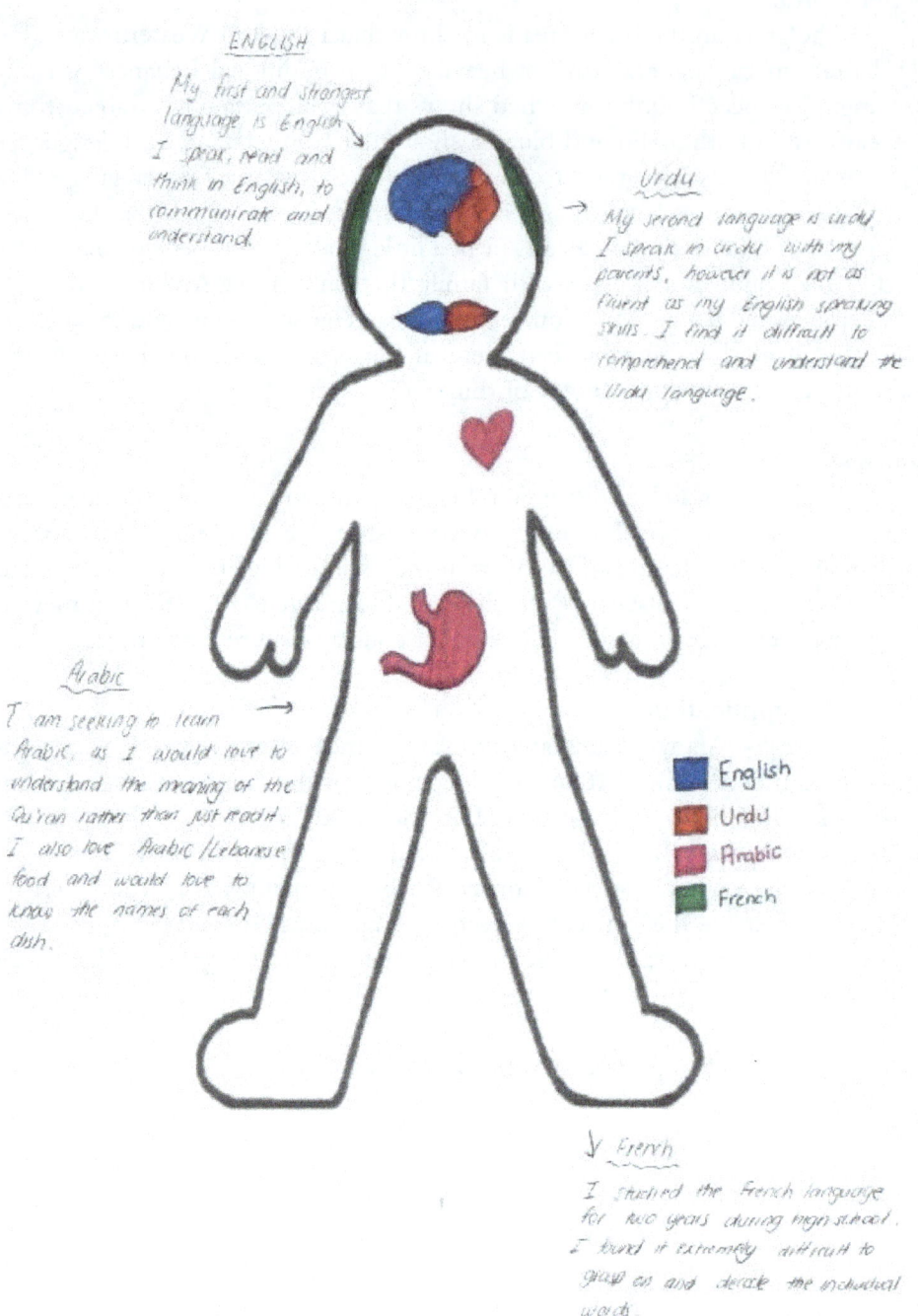

Aayah is a 22-year old female student who speaks English and Urdu at home, and learned French at school

In her words

English has been my strongest language since I was able to speak (Fig. 22). I am better able to express myself in English. I have used blue to draw in a part of the brain and mouth to illustrate the prominence of this language for me. My second language is Urdu; I speak Urdu with my parents. I have used red for this language. I seek to learn Arabic. Although I can read Arabic, I would love to understand the meaning of the Qu'ran, rather than just read it. I also love Arabic foods and would love to know the names of each dish. Thus, I have drawn in a stomach and heart using pink, my favourite colour.

Our response

Each language Aayah knows serves a unique function. English (blue) is her 'strongest' language; Urdu (red, part of the brain and mouth) is spoken occasionally at home and although not fluently, is her language of communication with her grandparents; and Arabic is the language of the Qur'an and prayer.

Classroom application

Visual – Many participants allocated and differentiated languages to brain or heart. The brain here is occupied by the dominant language, but the heart is 'filled' with her heritage language. In this case, the language of her religion is the language of her heart.

AGO – List all your aims, goals and objectives for learning a language. What does it require to attain your goals? List these. Plan how you might use your time and resources to achieve your goals.

Keywords: Urdu, French, family, Muslim, cuisine, identity

Figure 23. Sehrish is a 22-year old female student who speaks Arabic, English and Farsi at home, and learned Spanish at school.

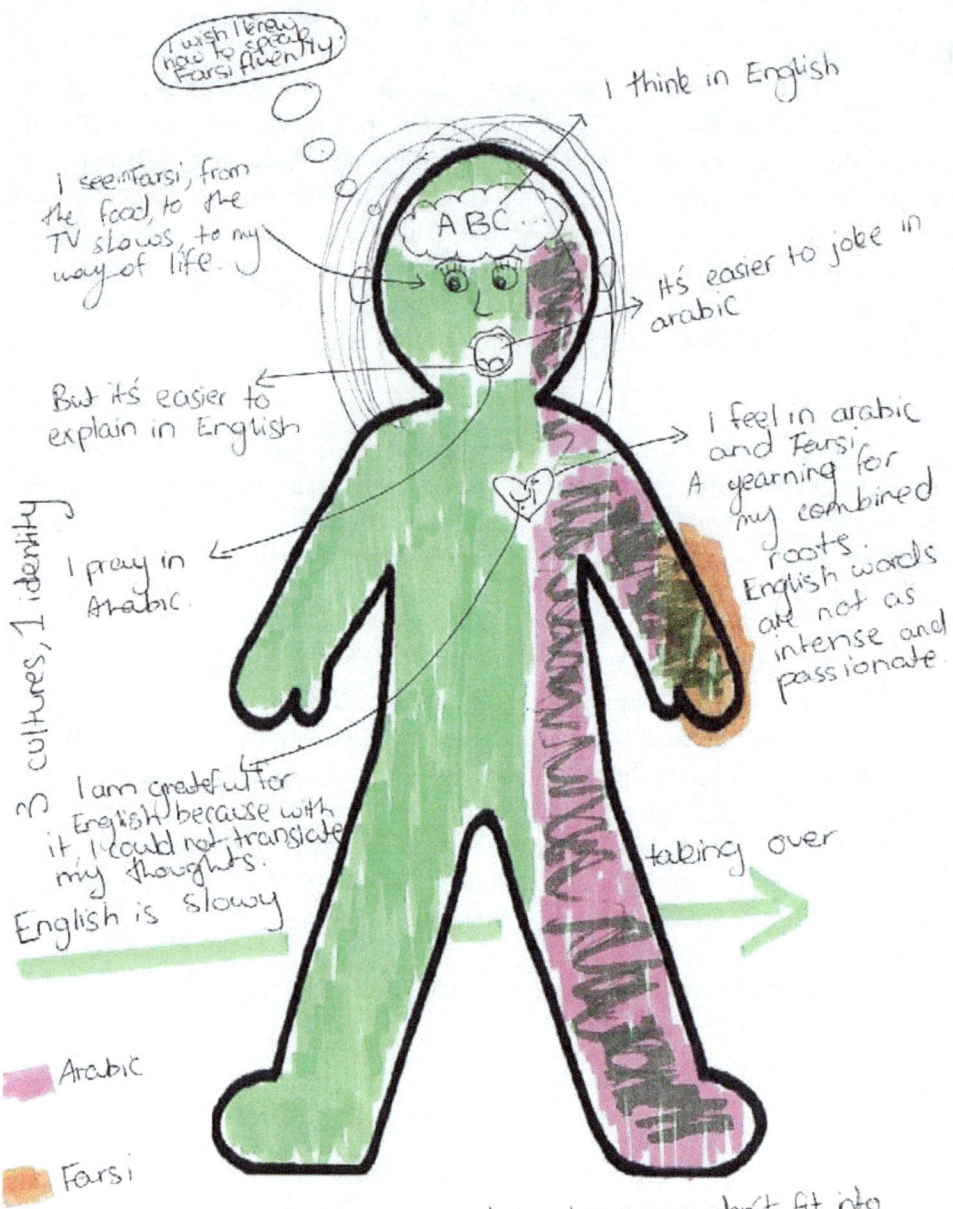

Sehrish is a 22-year old female student who speaks Arabic, English and Farsi at home, and learned Spanish at school.

In her words

My silhouette highlights how English is slowly taking over as my only dominant language (Fig. 23). My Arabic is slowly fading away and my Farsi is almost non-existent. I pray in Arabic; I feel in Arabic and Farsi - a yearning for my combined roots. I find it easier to tell a joke in Arabic - it sounds more humorous in that tongue. On the other hand, I find it easier to express my thoughts, feelings, fears and dreams in English due to having a larger vocabulary. I think in English; I see in Farsi, from foods... to my way of life.

Our response

Sehrish is acutely aware of the dominance of English in her communicative repertoire. She 'wishes to speak Farsi fluently', has a 'yearning for her combined roots' in Farsi and Arabic, and is conscious of her outsider status, of not 'fitting into anywhere – 'being too Australian to be Iraqi, being too Iraqi to be Iranian, and being too Iranian to be Australian, the never-ending cycle'. She thinks in English, has a perspective which is coloured by her Iranian heritage and responds emotionally in Arabic – 'three cultures, one identity'.

Classroom application

Visual – It is common for participants to divide up the body by languages (through the use of colours or patterns) to indicate which language(s) dominates. And in this drawing, the participant also indicates one language (English) is taking over.

CAF – What does it mean to be Iraqi, Iranian or Australian? What is identity? Can you have more than one identity? Can different identities merge in the one person? Why/Why not? What are the consequences of losing a part of your ethnic identity? What are the consequences of losing a heritage language?

Keywords: Arabic, Farsi, Spanish, identity, language loss, cuisine

Figure 24. Ava is a 22-year old English speaker, learned French in school and from Duolingo, and also German from school.

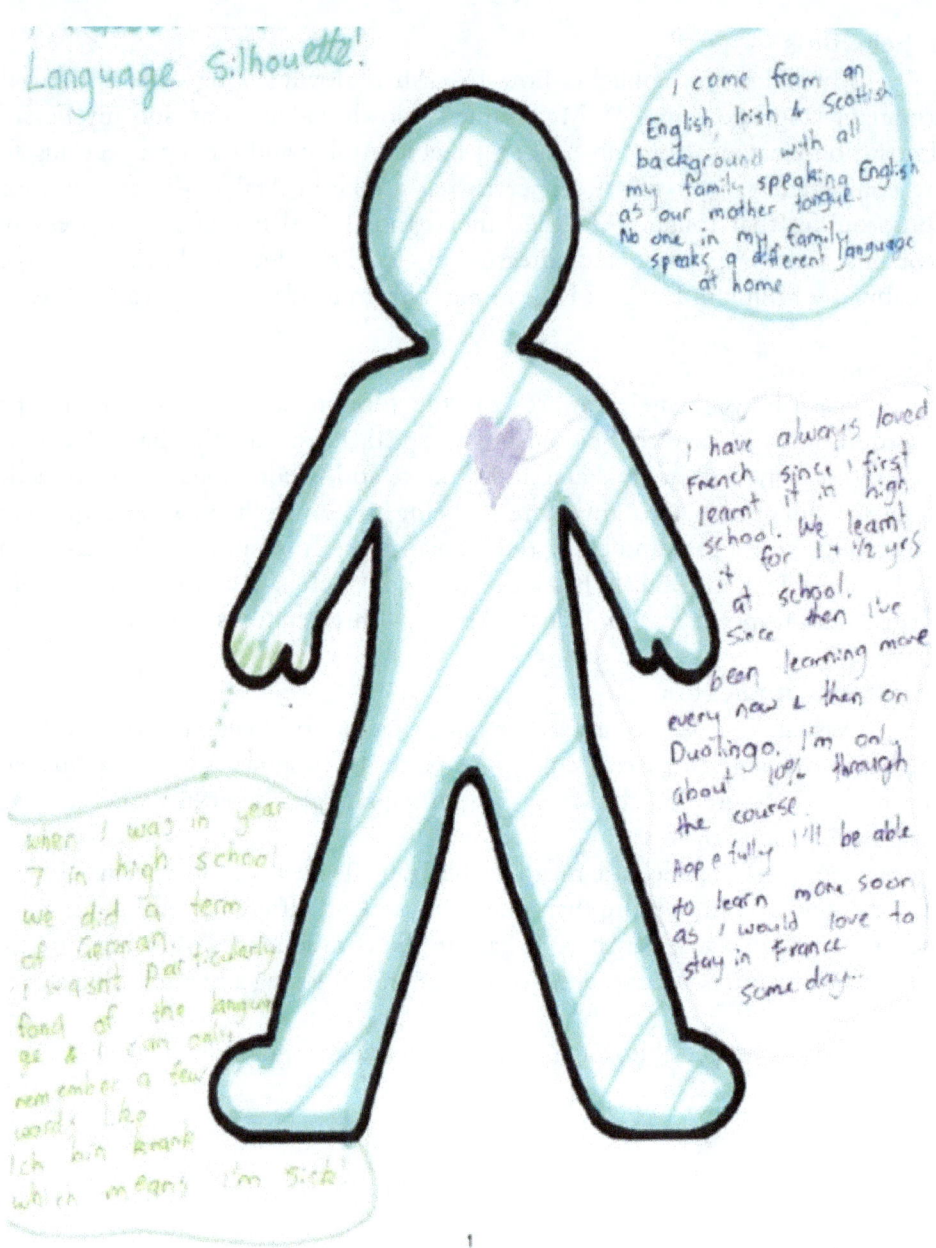

Ava is a 22-year old English speaker, learned French in school and from Duolingo, and also German from school.

In her words

I coloured the majority of my silhouette blue to represent my dominant language of English (Fig. 24). The green section of my silhouette near my fingers was coloured to depict the small amount of German I learnt in high school. I only remember a few key phrases - such as *Ich bin krank* (I am sick). This language is not one I am especially fond of, hence its distant position from the rest of my body. I learned French for one and a half years in school, and I deeply connected with this language. I consistently performed very well in my French class, eventually topping my grade.

Our response

Ava's introduction to French in High School was a positive experience and led her to believe she has a 'natural affinity for the language'. She 'adores' it, finds 'the sounds and flow to be quite beautiful' and performed quite well in it at school. PIt gave her the impetus to continue French language studies through self-study.

Classroom application

FIP – Define your priorities for learning your language of choice. What targets for language development can you set? Apart from apps, how else might you further language learning at the social level?

Keywords: French, German, family, travel, school, self-study

Figure 25. Sally is a 32-year old female student who speaks English, Malay and Arabic at home, and learned French in school.

Sally is a 32-year old female student who speaks English, Malay and Arabic at home, and learned French in school.

In her words

I am of mixed heritage; my first language is English (Fig. 25). My Mum did begin teaching me the basics of Malay (Bahasa Malaya) as a toddler, (but) largely out of worry that I may become 'confused', Mum stopped teaching me Malay. I've placed Malay at the core of my heart to symbolise the yearning that I have to, one day, share in the joy of speaking Malay with my Mum. The meshed orange colour scheme was chosen to show my partial knowledge of Malay. My eyes are searching for my 'forgotten Malay culture'. The heart encapsulates Arabic and English. The way I conduct myself spiritually is with the help of Arabic, as my Mum raised me a Muslim. My thoughts and my conversations are in English. The green symbolises how soothing, natural and easy English is for me.

Our response

Sally typifies the consequences to one's heritage language development when parental anxiety regarding children's mainstream language development leads them to stop instruction in home languages. The 'worry' the mother experienced, that her child may be 'confused' with two language systems, meant she prioritised instruction in English. As an adult, Sally now manifests a 'yearning' for fluency in Malay, her mother's language.

Classroom application

OPV – What are your parents' views about heritage language learning? Do you value the learning of that language? Do you think it is important to learn the language? Why/Why not? List some of your arguments. Provide examples to illustrate these points. What does the class think?

Keywords: Malay, Arabic, French, identity, heritage, Muslim, conflict

Figure 26. Caleb is a 20-year old male student who speaks English.

I used the brown because it represen[ts] a lack of diversit[y] as I have not learnt nor spo[ken] any languag[e] other than English.

Caleb is a 20-year old male student who speaks English.

In his words

I only know one language (English) – I coloured my person using a bleak beige pastel because it represents a lack of culturalism (Fig. 26). Only knowing one language, I sometimes feel I may not be as culturally diverse or experienced in comparison to other people. This may hinder my opportunities to work in rural or oversea areas.

Our response

Many of the pre-service teachers have a tug at the back of their mind that if they do not speak an additional language, eventually they may be disadvantaged. This may be true. However, while a little understanding of languages may not allow one to communicate like a native speaker of the language, yet this linguistic understanding may bring new perspectives and appreciation of the world, the cultures and their people.

Classroom application

PMI – Conduct a PMI on learning a new language. What does it take to be an adequate speaker of a language?

OPV – What are the experiences of those in your class who have mastery over another language? How do they assess the value of learning another language? How does that language competency influence their thinking and their interactions with others?

Keywords: English, conflict, disadvantaged

Figure 27. Elaine is a 24-year old female student who speaks English, and learned some Japanese in school and Vietnamese at work.

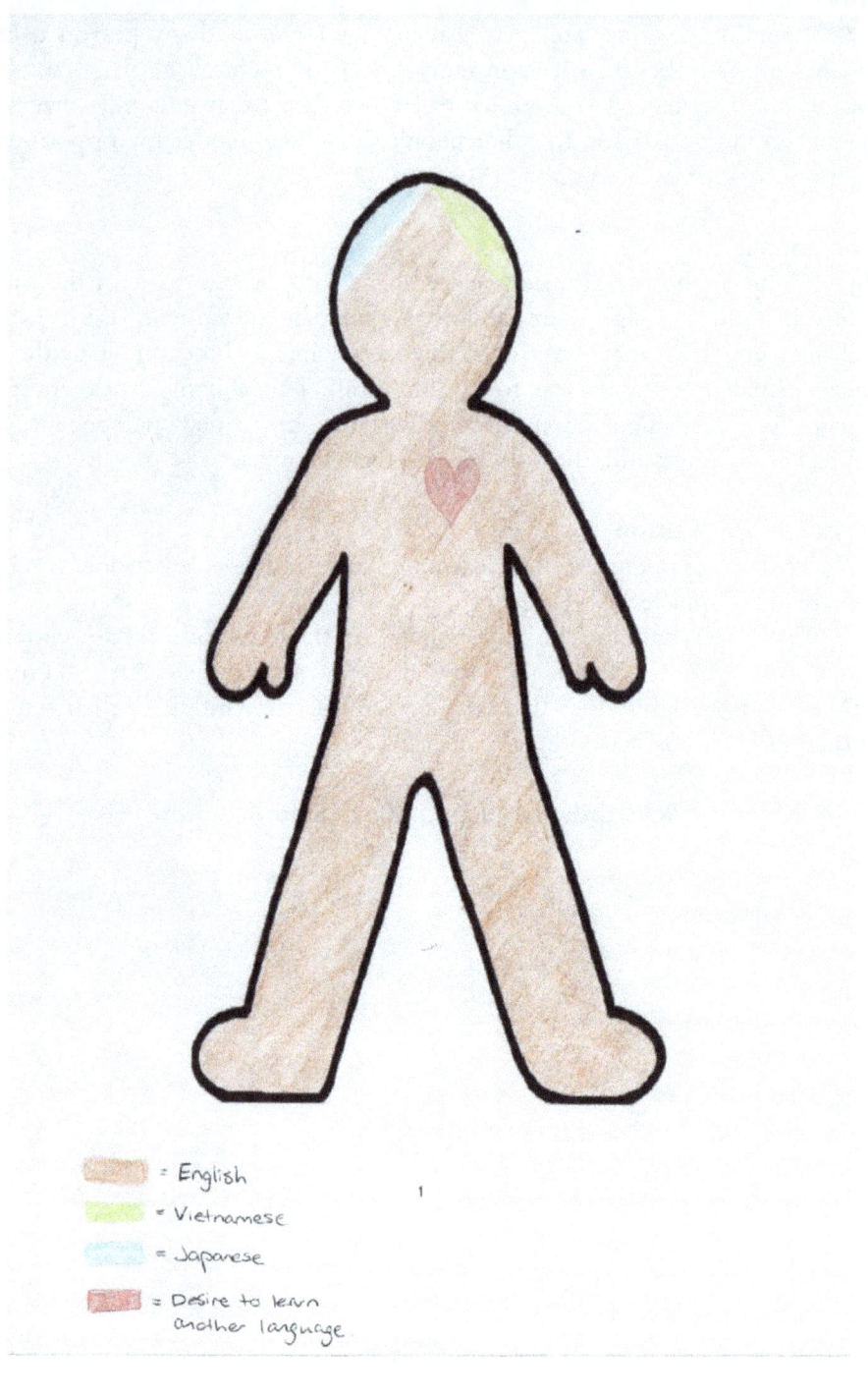

Elaine is a 24-year old female student who speaks English, and learned some Japanese in school and Vietnamese at work.

In her words

In high school, I studied Japanese for two terms (Fig. 27). During this time, I learnt only a handful of phrases. I learnt a little about the culture and the oral and written language. Unfortunately, I didn't continue learning this language so I know very little. By colouring a portion of my brain in blue (Japanese), this shows that I still have a small knowledge of the Japanese language. I have worked for a Vietnamese family for 4 years now and so have been exposed to the language (green brain). I can only speak a few phrases in Vietnamese though, as I haven't been able to match words and meanings together. I have a desire to learn another language, although I wouldn't know what language to learn (red heart). The rest of my silhouette is coloured in orange for English, my first and only language.

Our response

Elaine shows her desire to learn a new language, represented by a red heart in her silhouette. Her experiences so far have been unsatisfactory. A very limited exposure to Japanese at school and a longer period surrounded by Vietnamese have both resulted in the development of some language skills. She has not learnt foundational skills, or enough formal grammar or vocabulary to have facility with these languages.

Classroom application

Visual – It is unusual that the participant did not allocate a particular language for the heart but just say very vaguely 'a desire to learn another language'.

AGO – What language would you like to learn? Why do you want to learn that language? How will you turn your desire to action and acquisition? What avenues have you explored? Who will help you? Define your goals.

Keywords: Japanese, Vietnamese, workplace

Figure 28. Samuel is a 24-year old male student who speaks Vietnamese and English at home, learned French in school (Year 8), and continued to self-teach French, Russian and Norwegian (Bokmal).

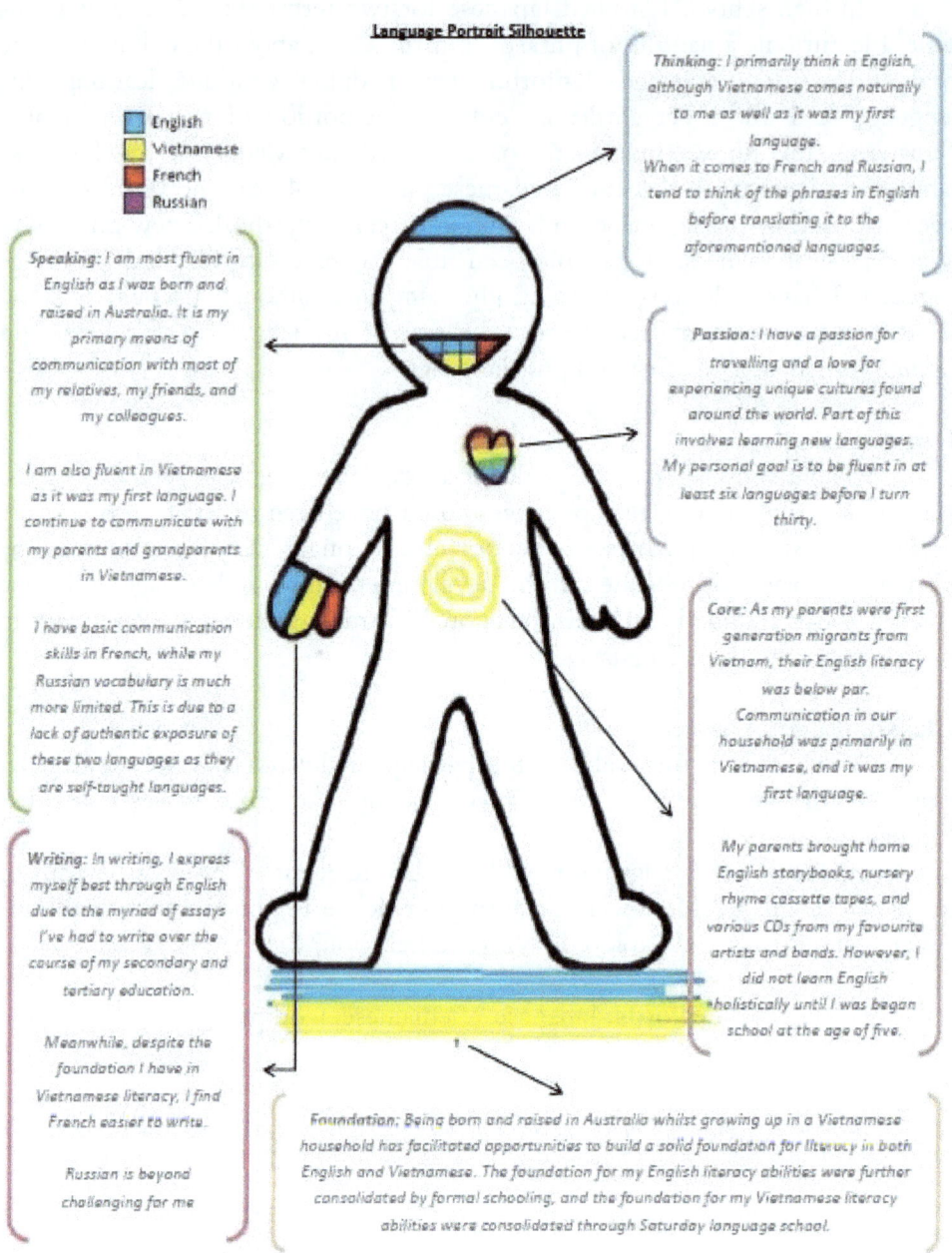

Samuel is a 24-year old male student who speaks Vietnamese and English at home, learned French in school (Year 8), and continued to self-teach French, Russian and Norwegian (Bokmal).

In his words

As my parents are first generation migrants from Vietnam, communication in our house is primarily in Vietnamese, and it is my first language (Fig. 28). The yellow spiral was drawn to represent my first language and the core of my parents' heritage which was fostered at a young age and continues to grow to this day. I communicate with my parents and grandparents in Vietnamese. The head is blue as English is my dominant language and I subconsciously think in English. The mouth is sectioned off like teeth, and the teeth are coloured strategically to represent my level of fluency in speaking in each language. For example, as I am most fluent and most comfortable with English, I have coloured three sections in blue. I have basic communication skills in French (red). Russian is my least spoken language, hence only one small section is coloured in purple.

Our response

Samuel has a 'passion' for languages and aims to be fluent in six languages by the time he is 30. An interest in French began with French language classes at school. Russian and Norwegian are self-taught and language competencies and these are developing. The foundations of his communicative repertoire, however, rest with Vietnamese and English. Vietnamese, the language of his parents, was fostered at the beginning of his life and continues to grow to this day. English was learnt primarily through formal schooling. While Vietnamese forms the core of his being, Samuel thinks and writes mainly in English.

Classroom application

Visual – Some participants prefer to write directly next to the portraits for explanation. And this is an example of very detailed explanation.

PMI – Do a PMI to assess the approach taken here to study three new languages at the same time.

FIP – What are your priorities when learning a new language? What is essential to the learning of a new language? How would you identify and meet the learning needs for each language in order to acquire fluency in each of your chosen languages?

Keywords: Vietnamese, French, Russian, Norwegian, Bokmal, travel, heritage, self-taught

Figure 29. Sona is a 21-year old female student who speaks Hindi and English at home.

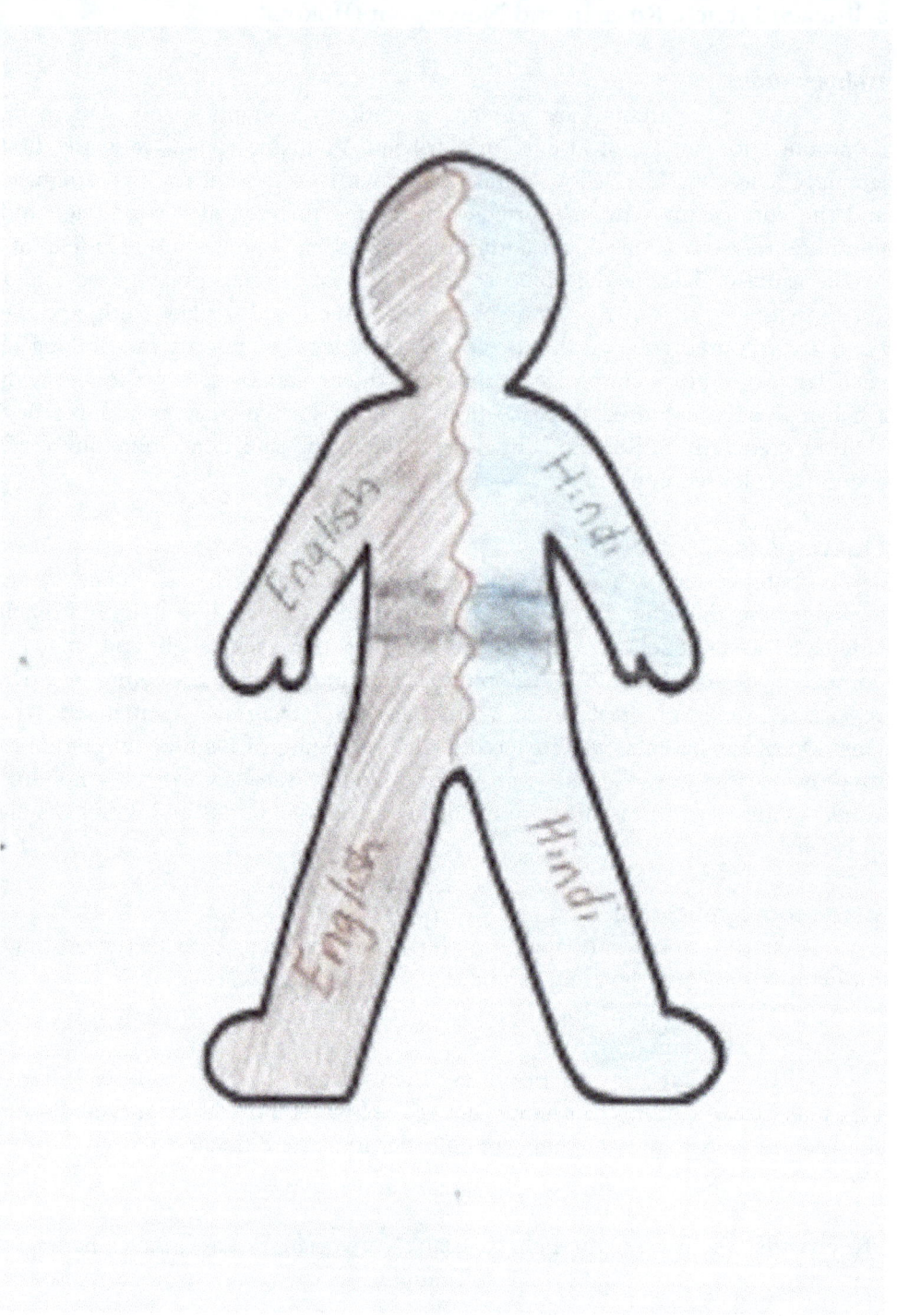

Sona is a 21-year old female student who speaks Hindi and English at home.

In her words

I grew up speaking two languages (Fig. 29). When I was young, my parents spoke to me in Hindi as well as in English. Just before I entered school, my parents spoke to me in English so that I was prepared in the classroom. As I developed my English in school, my parents spoke to me only in Hindi. They always told me that it was important to speak in your mother tongue, as they wanted me to teach my children to speak in Hindi. English is my main language, as I speak this language most of the time. I only ever speak in Hindi to my parents. These languages form my identity. This is why my language silhouette portrait is divided into two - Hindi and English.

Our response

As a consequence of her parents' insistence on home language maintenance, Sona is able to communicate fluently in Hindi. She does however admit that due to the fact that her communicative partners in Hindi are limited to her parents, her Hindi language development has remained behind English, the language of school, her academic work and the mainstream community. Despite the fact that she sees herself as the product of both, her heritage and her western influences, Sona has come to believe that her English language skills and the western influences in her life, will eventually comprise her dominant self.

Classroom application

Visual – It is common for participants to divide up the body by languages (through the use of colours or patterns) to indicate which language(s) dominates, or if there is a balance.

CAF – How might you use your heritage language outside the home? Do you think this is important to language development? Why? Is it important to learn to read and write in a language which you hope to pass on to the next generation? Why do you hold that view? Do others in class hold a different view? Are academic competencies in the language of the home important to develop?

Keywords: Hindi, identity

Figure 30. Esther is a 27-year old female student who taught herself Spanish through Duolingo.

Esther is a 27-year old female student who taught herself Spanish through Duolingo.

In her words

The red and dark blue of the Union Jack represents English (Fig. 30). English is the only language I knew growing up, and I think, speak, and write in it fluently - to such a high degree of fluency that I currently work as a writer and editor (see the red-and-blue pencil). The dark green and gold surrounding the Union Jack in the speech bubble represents the Australian accent and dialect of English that I speak. However, my heart's desire is to travel the world, to fly across the sky and connect with other cultures, represented by the heart, coloured in light blue to represent the colour of the sky. I desire to learn other languages so that I can do this. Light lime green represents Spanish, the first language that I have deliberately tried to learn independently of my schooling. I chose lime green because it is the colour of the Duolingo app through which I am learning the language. I connect with the language through an app on my phone, and this is where I hear the new language that is starting to permeate my thoughts as well (which is why a small amount of lime green can also be seen in my 'brain', overlaying the red and dark blue representation of English).

Our response

This is a modern response to the lack of language learning opportunities. Many people may encounter a similar issue – limited or no access to language education in formal schooling and expensive language courses for adults. However, there are a number of free language learning and language exchange platforms/apps available online. These platforms and apps may be a positive step for anyone who wants to start learning a language. But languages, by their very essence, demand communicative exchanges with others. It is important to go beyond tools and incorporate people interactions using the language medium for communication.

Classroom application

Visual – It is clever the way the participant shows the speaking of two languages: English and Spanish in one speech bubble. Others have used multiple speech bubbles for different languages.

CAF – What are other ways you can add to your learning strategies to accelerate the pace of your language acquisition? Before you travel overseas, could you develop your skills in a language by using the people resources present in this country?

Keywords: Spanish, school, technology

Figure 31. James is a 25-year old male student who speaks English, Lebanese Arabic and French at home, learned Italian from YouTube and his partner, and Korean from Internet and friends.

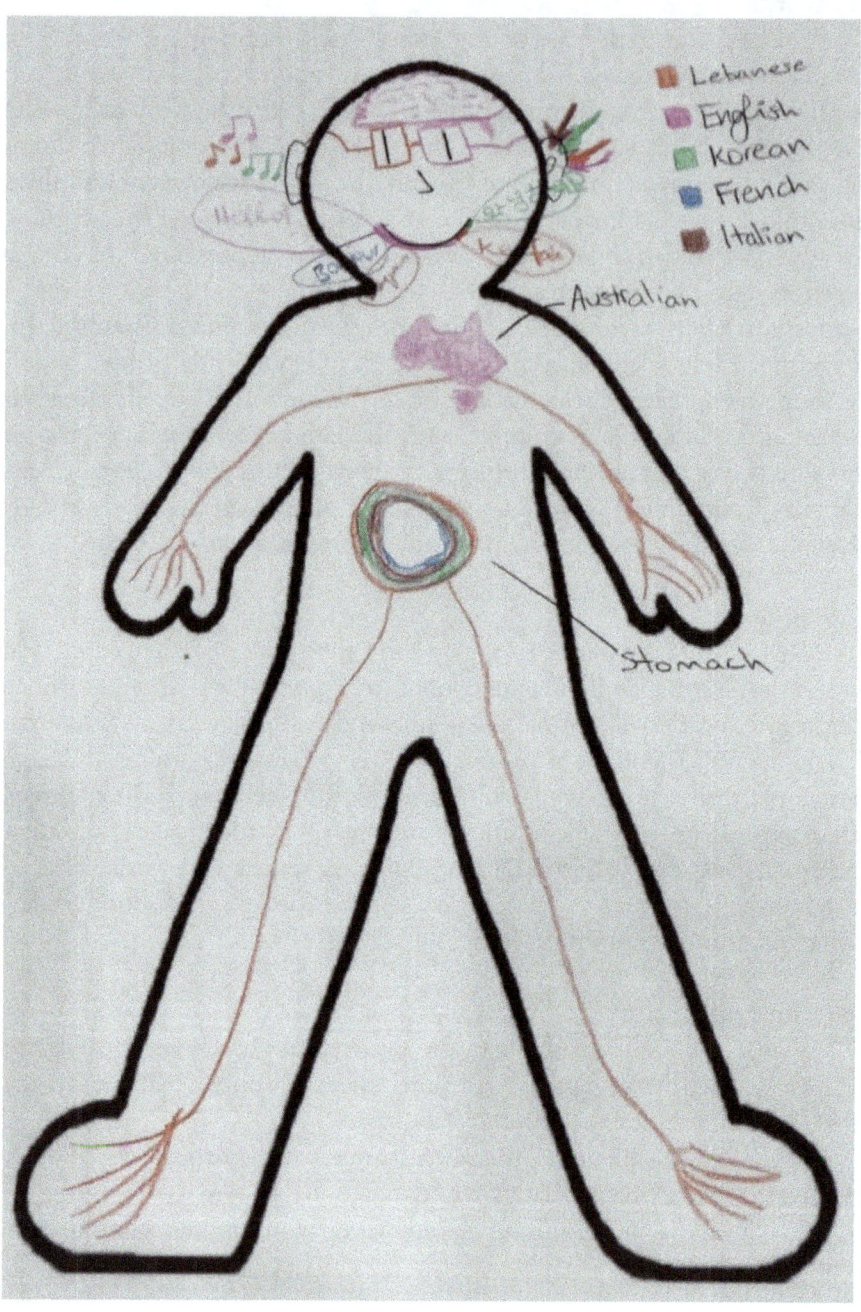

James is a 25-year old male student who speaks English, Lebanese Arabic and French at home, learned Italian from YouTube and his partner, and Korean from Internet and friends.

In his words

English is my main language (I think in it too) hence the purple brain (Fig. 31). I can speak a bit of Arabic and even less Korean, and even less Italian and French - hence the greetings in those languages. I see/hear my relatives and parents speaking in Lebanese Arabic and I understand them most of the time. I listen to Arabic, Korean and English music. Although 'Australian' isn't a language, my heart is Australia as I am Australian, born and raised here, played cricket, football, and rugby league throughout my childhood and adolescence and identify as an Australian. The red veins indicate Lebanese blood as both parents are Lebanese and I feel a strong connection with my heritage – I wish to learn more though I complained as a child to learn Arabic.

Our response

James sees and hears his parents and extended family speak Arabic. In his veins, he believes, flow 'Lebanese blood', and he has a 'strong connection' with his heritage. At the same time, James notes that he regrets he can speak only a 'little' Arabic and wishes he'd made use of the opportunities for language learning in his childhood. At the time, 'I complained as a child to learn Arabic'.

Classroom application

Visual – The map of Australia is an unusual symbol of the heart which indicates the participant's affiliation with being Australian. The greetings in different languages refer to his superficial vocabulary acquisition and regret for not having acquired deeper language skills, including the loss of much of his heritage language. The silhouette lends itself to natural symbolism, such as the heart, stomach and veins to express thoughts and feelings about the meaning of language and heritage.

CAF and APC – What advice would you give someone about the best ways to maintain their heritage language, (or, learn other languages), starting from young childhood? Consider different opportunities and choices which you would find most valuable.

Planning – One way to learn other languages is through technology and the media. If you were to plan a language program, what would you include? (E.g. YouTube, the Internet, language apps, films, audio-tapes, blogs, etc.).

CAF – How would you define identity? Is it one or many things?

Keywords: Arabic, French, Italian, Korean, YouTube, family, friends, music

Figure 32. Theresa is a 22-year old female student who speaks English and Seychellois Creole, and learned French and Japanese in school, and Spanish from friend.

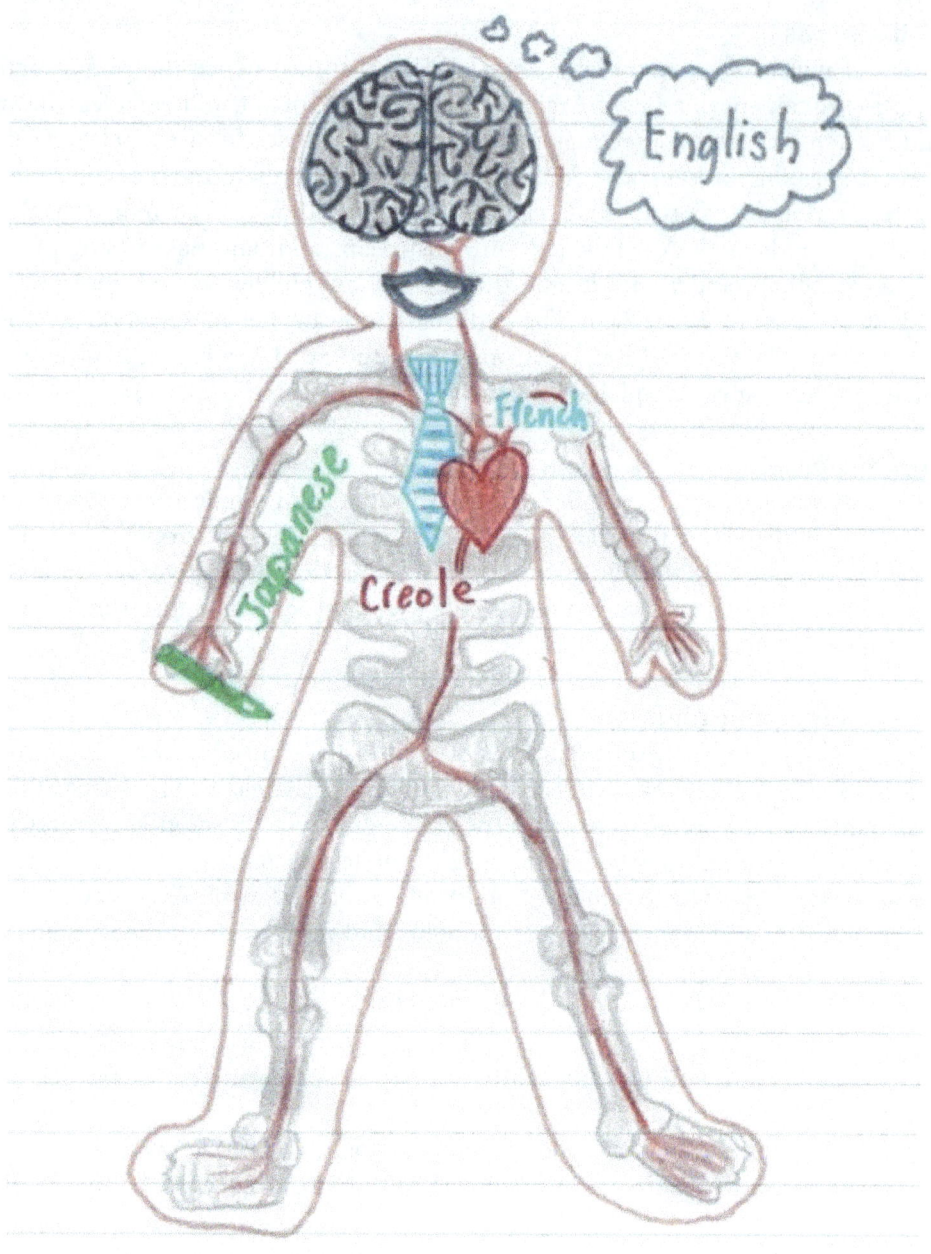

Theresa is a 22-year old female student who speaks English and Seychellois Creole, and learned French and Japanese in school, and Spanish from friend.

In her words

The mouth and brain are drawn in grey to represent that I speak and think in English (Fig. 32). I have also drawn the skeletal system in grey as my father's side is of strong British Isles descent - it's in my bones! I have drawn my heart and blood flow in red to represent my Seychellois heritage. The colour red because of its association with passion, feelings and emotion, which reflects the Seychellois culture of strong displays and feelings of emotion.

Our response

Theresa's 'passion, feelings and emotion' lie with her Seychellois heritage and the Seychellois Creole language. The language is represented in red and courses through her heart and blood. But Theresa thinks in English, which is her father's heritage.

Classroom application

Visual – This is an unusual drawing, incorporating finer details of a skeleton, with strong bones representing paternal heritage, and the heart and blood, her maternal side. When a very simple body outline is given, participants can be encouraged to be creative in their use of visual metaphor.

PMI – *Language and culture define who we are*. Use a PMI to examine this statement.

CAF – What are the things you love most about your heritage language/s and culture/s? List these and consider less obvious ones you might have left out. Compare with others.

AGO – If you have strong foundations in your heritage language, how can this assist you in learning new languages?

Keywords: Seychellois, Creole, French, Japanese, Spanish, friends, family

Figure 33. Linda is a 21-year old female student who learned Japanese in school, and Norwegian during her travel.

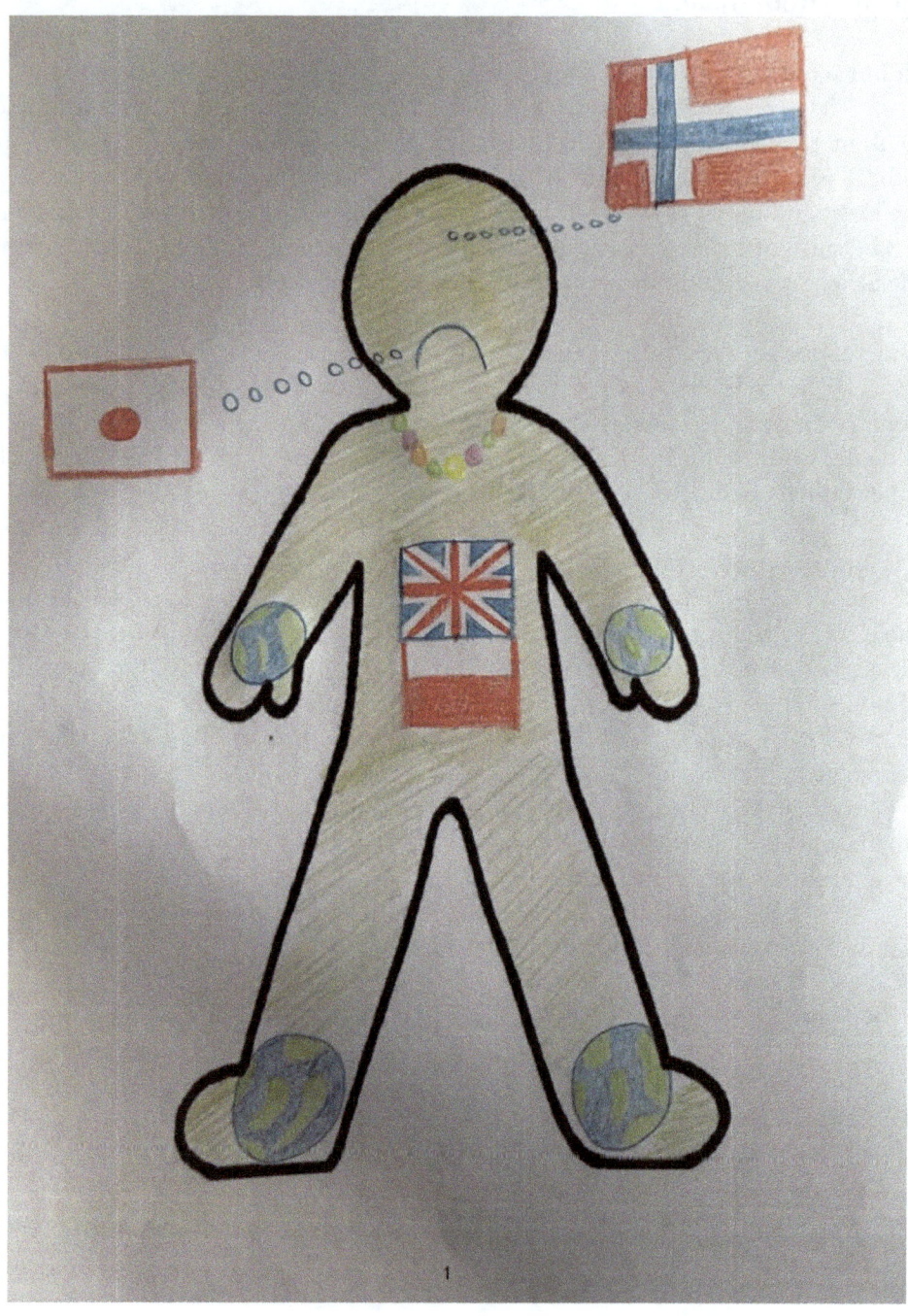

Linda is a 21-year old female student who learned Japanese in school, and Norwegian during her travel.

In her words

The British and Polish flag in the middle of my silhouette represent my heritage on both sides of my family (Fig. 33). The 'earths' on my hands and feet represent the 20+ countries I have travelled to and multiple languages I have heard. The Japanese flag connected to a 'sad face' represents the loss of the language I learnt at school as I have grown older and the Norwegian flag connected to my brain reflects myself currently trying to learn the language for overseas university exchange. My body is faintly coloured in gold and green to represent living in Australia. Finally, the multiple colours around my neck reflect the many friends I have around the world, including from South Africa and China and the diverse cultures and languages I have experienced through them.

Our response

Linda's experience may be a very familiar story for many people. She learned some Japanese at school, but the infrequent use means she no longer has the same level of competence and connection. But now she has a different life goal – to learn Norwegian for her student exchange. At different stages in life, many people will have different goals and connections, and in many cases, languages may be involved. It could be learning Italian for a trip-of-a-lifetime, or Korean for TV dramas, or Gaelic to connect with family members. We may be attached to languages and cultures at different points of our lives, and the learning will continue.

Classroom application

Visual – The silhouette reads like a map which draws together the participant's involvement in a larger multicultural world. The Australian flag at the centre establishes her identity and the two flags at either side of her head reflect her language experiences of loss and new acquisition in the future. The topic of future language goals and reasons for them, is an interesting topic for teachers to consider.

AGO – What is identity? Is it possible for identity to change? Consider different experiences in your life which might have influenced this.

AGO – What are your goals for the future? How does your understanding of different languages contribute to this picture?

CAF and FIP – When you decide to learn a new language what are the most important factors you need to consider? What other factors would motivate you, as well?

Keywords: Polish, Japanese, Norwegian, travel, language loss

Figure 34. Agatha is a 35-year old female student who speaks English and Tagalog at home, and learned Japanese at Technical and Further Education (TAFE) and also while living in Japan.

Agatha is a 35-year old female student who speaks English and Tagalog at home, and learned Japanese at Technical and Further Education (TAFE) and also while living in Japan.

In her words

The kanji character "日" used in Japanese (Fig. 34), and which stands for Japanese, is drawn with an arrow towards ear, arrow away from mouth and in one of the thought bubbles represents my Japanese language abilities – in listening, speaking and internal thought processes (although I am not a native speaker). The red, circle-like heart resembles the rising sun of the Japanese flag and is meant to represent my personal connection to the Japanese language and culture. Due to this connection and interest in the language I was able to have many meaningful experiences and develop wonderful friendships and even the relationship with my husband.

Our response

Agatha first acquired her language competencies in Japanese through her studies in Technical and Further Education (TAFE) and by living in Japan. These were her early experiences with Japanese. Subsequently, Agatha has developed her language skills in Japanese with her partner and friends. Her language is developed enough for her to speak, understand and think in Japanese.

Classroom application

Visual – The head of the silhouette, surrounded by Japanese characters, indicates the participant's proficiency in speaking Japanese, a language learnt later in life. Her intense emotional attachment to the Japanese language is symbolised by the heart covered by an image of the rising sun. However, both arms are covered in the Philippines flag, a reference to her heritage language and culture. Silhouettes can create an intimate picture of each individual's changing life portrait.

CAF – If you were to give advice to someone who is about to learn a new language, what would you say are the best practices that worked for you?

OPV – How can learning a new language and developing knowledge of that culture help you understand other people's points of view? Discuss together with examples.

Keywords: Japanese, TAFE, culture

Figure 35. Helen is a 23-year old female student who wants to learn Aboriginal Languages.

Helen is a 23-year old female student who wants to learn Aboriginal Languages.

In her words

I wrote 'English' throughout the majority of my silhouette as this was my first language and it is the only one I know fluently (Fig. 35). In brown small writing I wrote, "Italian, French and German" as they were superficially taught to me at High School each for a term so I never was able to immerse myself in these languages. My eyes are multi-coloured as I see the richness and diversity of language and how it shows such expression and culture in other people, which I love. My heart however is purple and the purple connects to my thoughts that I have had for a long time, a yearning to learn an Indigenous language and my shock and surprise that I never got the opportunity to learn and immerse myself in it and get to appreciate it. I tried to learn an Indigenous language at university as a major at one point but it was not offered. Throughout my education course I am really disheartened that we have never been taught one of the Aboriginal and Torres Strait Islander (ATSI) languages, even though as future teachers we will teach students of ATSI backgrounds.

Our response

With the new Australian curriculum framework for Aboriginal Languages still being worked out in New South Wales, it will good to know that some pre-service teachers are preparing themselves for this new challenge. There are many community-based Aboriginal Language courses provided by tertiary institutes and community organizations.

Classroom application

Visual – The multi-coloured eyes in the silhouette indicate 'the richness and diversity' of languages and cultures which the participant yearns to experience. Her strong desire to learn an Aboriginal language is shown by the connection between the purple heart and clouds. The silhouette provides a vehicle to voice her frustration about restricted educational opportunities to learn local languages relevant to her future.

FIP – Many people wish to have stronger skills in their heritage language or long to learn new languages. This might include local community or Indigenous languages. What are the languages you would like to learn in the future? What are the first steps you can take to make this happen?

AGO – What are your goals in life? What challenges would you set for yourself to achieve these goals?

PMI – *A new language can be learnt in a 100 hour.* Conduct a PMI on this statement.

Keywords: Italian, French, German, Aboriginal Languages, school

Figure 36. Katarina is a 22-year old female student who speaks English and Chinese at home, majored in Croatian in university, learned Italian in school, and taught herself Spanish.

Katarina is a 22-year old female student who speaks English and Chinese at home, majored in Croatian in university, learned Italian in school, and taught herself Spanish.

In her words

I used the colour red symbolise Chinese (Fig. 36). This is the language that is spoken to me at home; however, I respond in English. I have also used this colour in the heart to symbolise my heritage as my mother is Chinese and this is very close to my heart. Alongside Chinese, I have used a blue similar to that seen on the flag of Croatia to symbolise my father's side. From the ages of 4 to 15, I participated in a Croatian dance group where we would sing traditional Croatian songs in addition to dance. Whilst I did not understand the lyrics, I developed very good pronunciation from an early age. I've since completed 4 years of Croatian at university. Spanish is represented in yellow. This is a language I've had a strong desire to learn and recently I've started to teach myself the language through an app as well as from friends.

Our response

Katarina began her language development learning English and Chinese simultaneously, at the same pace. However, with the start of formal schooling, she experienced 'language loss' with English language development outpacing Chinese to the extent that she lost her productive skills in Chinese and now her Chinese language skills are confined to receptive abilities: 'I have only been able to understand Chinese and respond in English'. Katarina has also devoted time to studying her father's language, Croatian. She began by learning Croatian dance and songs from the ages of 4-15, and pursued university studies in Croatian.

Classroom application

Visual – Shades of colour across the body indicate the levels of importance of multiple languages in the participant's life. Her maternal and paternal heritage is symbolised by the dual colours of the heart. Her mother's heritage language is represented by a thin band of red, in contrast to the larger representation of English at the top of the head. The silhouette can give expression to students' feelings about loss of heritage language.

CAF – Consider the many ways in which heritage language can be kept 'alive' outside the home. List your ideas and discuss which are the most appealing to you and why. Aim to include as many ideas as possible.

C&S – How can knowledge of your heritage language and other languages be of value to you now and in the future? Or, what would be the consequences of losing your heritage language now and in the future?

Keywords: Chinese, Croatian, Italian, Spanish, emotion, heritage, university

Figure 37. Dan is a 21-year old male student who learned some Korean at school, and Hindu and Urdu when playing hockey with friends.

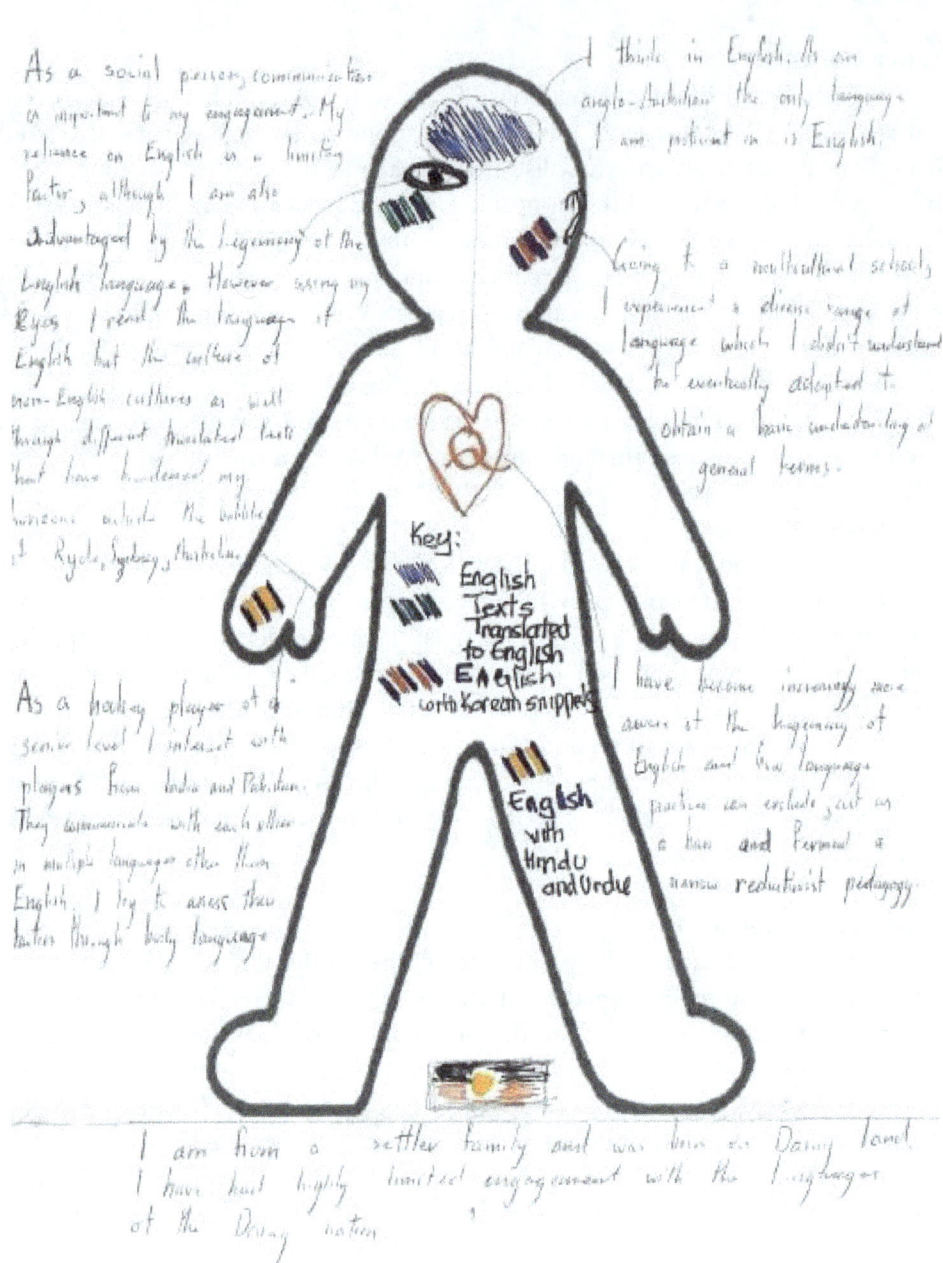

Dan is a 21-year old male student who learned some Korean at school, and Hindu and Urdu when playing hockey with friends.

In his words

My language silhouette reflects the hegemony of the English language in my environmental contexts (Fig. 37). I was born into an English language family and my first language was English. Although born on the land of the Darug nation, I have had almost no exposure to Darug language. While I am intellectually aware of the struggles of Aboriginal Australians, their languages are external to me (the Aboriginal flag). English (blue) dominates my consciousness. Korean (red) phrases learnt at school through friends. Hindu and Urdu phrases (orange) spoken by players in hockey settings and texts that I know have been translated into English are represented as green. These colours of green, red and orange are presented in a variegated way, intersected with blue, showing my interaction with them is mediated by the primacy of English in my consciousness and in the presented contexts.

Our response

Dan shows a complex, strongly emotional response to his limited exposure to other languages, most specifically one of Australia's own indigenous languages, Darug. He writes that he has "…become increasingly aware of the hegemony of English and how language practices exclude, act as a ban and ferment a narrow reductionist pedagogy". His regret is that lack of exposure to non-English speaking cultures and translated texts has limited his horizons beyond his own small local world (symbolised by a single, glaring eye).

Classroom application

Visual – Students have different learning styles and ways of expressing their ideas and feelings. They might lean towards more verbal or visual forms of expression. This silhouette is crowded with written notes which explain the participant's thoughts and beliefs about the relevance of languages denied him in his local world, particularly Indigenous languages. Teachers can encourage students to combine a variety of different mediums to express their ideas.

APC – (Series of related questions). Are we defined by the dominant language of our society? What other languages would you like to learn which could be of value in developing your local world worldview? How could opportunities to learn these languages be advantageous to you in your future life and career? (E.g. Indigenous languages, community languages, etc.).

OPV – Can knowledge of different languages and cultures develop deeper perspectives and understanding of other people's points of view? Discuss, using different examples.

Keywords: Korean, Hindi, Urdu, sports, friends, Darug, Aboriginal Languages

Figure 38. Paul is a 41-year old male student who speaks English and German at home, and learned Japanese in high school.

Paul is a 41-year old male student who speaks English and German at home, and learned Japanese in high school.

In his words

Blue at the top of the head to represent English (Fig. 38), which is the predominant language spoken at home growing up; green ears for Polish being spoken by mother and grandmother on some occasions which I regret not learning; red mouth for Japanese learnt in High School; German flag for the heart as my wife is from Germany and our 6-year-old son is learning both English and German; purple hands to show that I learned to communicate with people speaking other languages through gestures as well as words in my 10 years in a Backpackers Hostel and coloured feet to show travelling where I learned about many cultures and Languages.

Our response

Paul grew up in a linguistically diverse environment. His mother and grandmother spoke Polish on 'some occasions'; they also spoke English. In high school, Paul learnt Japanese. He 'regrets' not taking the opportunity to learn Polish but has tried to ensure that his own son maintains his link to German, the language of his mother and Paul's wife. Paul himself has been learning German for the last six years. It is the language of his heart. This leads to an interesting question: why do people learn particular languages? Does one learn a language because a parent speaks it? What makes Paul value German and expend so much time in learning it?

Classroom application

Visual – Many participants drew and coloured their hearts with colours associated with their attachment to their heritage languages and cultures. In this case, the participant drew the German flag, which is not his own home language, to represent his emotional connection with the German language. Older student experiences and the influences of personal relationships could be an interesting area to discuss.

CAF – We live in a multicultural world. Consider the influences in your life which might have inspired you to learn another foreign language (e.g. friendships, family connections, travel, sport, etc.).

FIP – When you decide to learn a new language what are the most important factors to take into account?

C&S – How can your understanding and skills in speaking languages be of benefit to you now and in the future?

Keywords: German, Japanese, family, heritage, school, travel, gesture

Figure 39. Philip is a 24-year old male student who speaks English and Greek at home, and learned Italian in school.

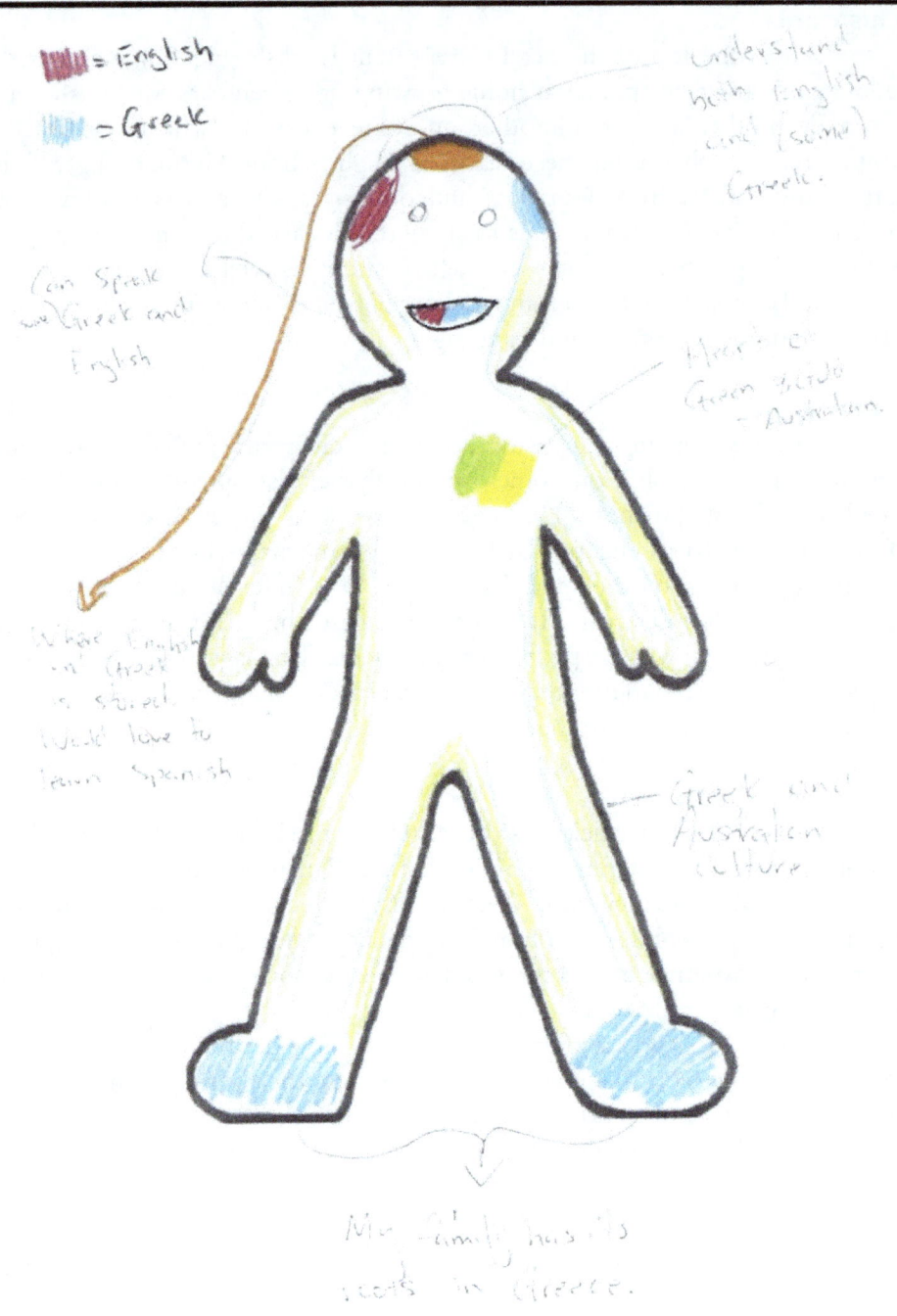

Philip is a 24-year old male student who speaks English and Greek at home, and learned Italian in school.

In his words

The feet of the silhouette are coloured blue illustrating that my family has its roots in Greece (Fig. 39). The heart area is coloured green and gold to represent my proud Australian identity. The mouth and ears represent English and Greek as a language. I can speak and understand both Greek and English. The border of the silhouette is coloured green, gold and blue to represent my Australian and Greek culture.

Our response

Philip understands and speaks both Greek and English. And while his heart is Australian, he states that his roots are all Greek. This is frequently the case for heritage language learners – they find their 'roots' in their heritage cultures but have developed a pan-Australian perspective.

Classroom application

Visual – The blue feet represent the participant's connection to his Greek heritage roots. The green and gold heart symbolises his feelings of belonging in Australia. Although Greek and English are equally represented, English is dominant in his life with Greek remaining in the background. Teachers can discuss the significant topic of heritage language and culture loss at the expense of fitting into mainstream society.

CAF – Think of all the things you love about your heritage language and culture. Make a list of these and consider how they fit together with your Australian identity.

AGO – What is identity? How do you define who you are in an Australian context? Where does heritage language and culture fit into this description?

FIP – If you are able to speak more than one language proficiently, how does this give you the confidence and skills to learn other languages? What advice would you give someone who is about to learn a new language?

Keywords: Greek, Italian, identity

Figure 40. Sevinc is a 24-year old female student who speaks English and Turkish at home.

Sevinc is a 24-year old female student who speaks English and Turkish at home.

In her words

My first language is English and to me it represents the colour blue (Fig. 40). The reason I have chosen the colour blue is because it is a colour of relaxation and something I believe I am good at. The language used by my family is Turkish and the reason why I believe it represents the colour green to me is because it is exciting. When I hear the different ways things are said in Turkish I am always amused. It is different to English; in some instances, there seems to be more depth in words. Slang is a "language" I have picked up through everyday conversations with friends. I associate slang with red because it does seem a little rebellious.

Our response

When some heritage language learners express their relationships with their home languages, they frequently talk about an excitement that comes with an intimate knowledge of the language. When they use the heritage language, they are communicating in codes with their community members. This could be an initial step to excite our young learners.

Classroom application

Visual – The silhouette vibrates with neon lit colours. These vibrant blues, greens and reds express the participant's feelings, dominated by green, her allegiance to her heritage language. Language produces visceral reactions of relaxation, excitement, amusement and rebellion. The relationship between languages and emotions is an interesting area for students to explore.

CAF – What are the things you love most about your heritage language and culture? List these, then discuss what defines your home language to you, what excites you most about it, or anything you feel strongly about.

APC – *Language is powerful because....* Finish this statement with as many alternatives as you can. Share ideas.

C&S and OPV – How would the ability to speak your heritage, or other languages, at an advanced level benefit your life now and in the future? How would diversity in language background help you to see other people's points of view?

Keywords: Turkish, slang, emotion, family

Figure 41. Tham is a 22-year old female student who speaks Vietnamese and English at home.

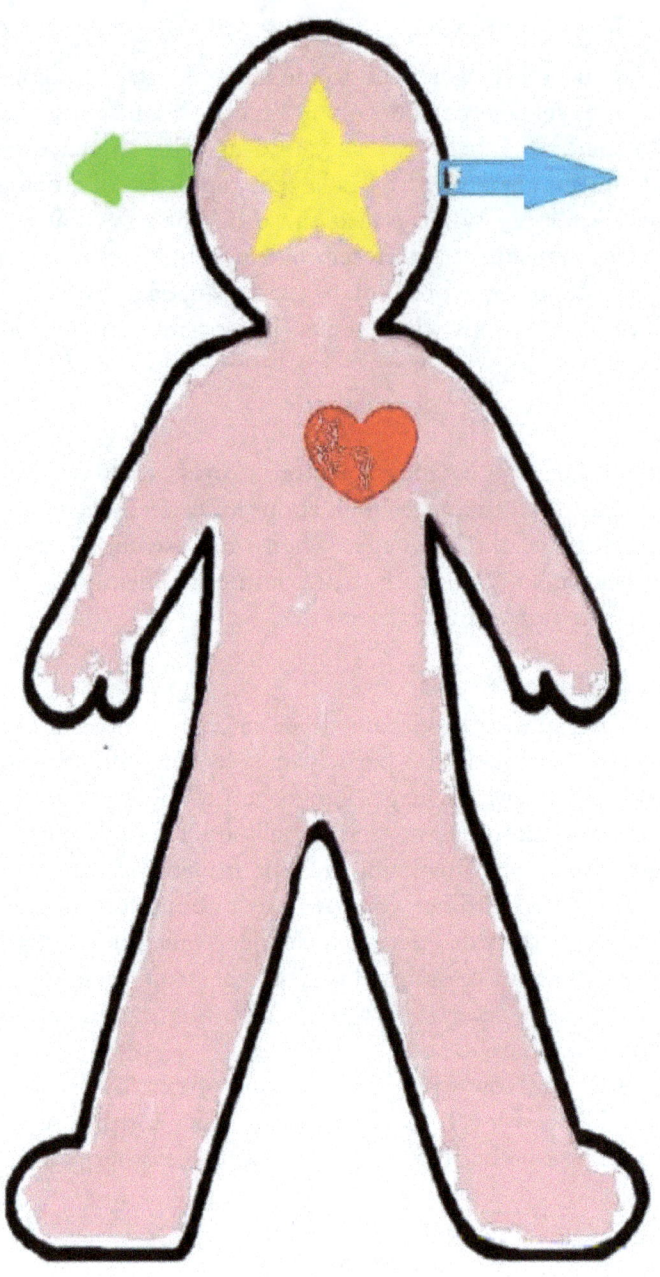

Tham is a 22-year old female student who speaks Vietnamese and English at home.

In her words

I coloured my entire silhouette pink as I am Vietnamese, my biological father is Vietnamese and my mum is Vietnamese (Fig. 41). I can speak and understand Vietnamese. I however, was born in Australia and I feel more Australian (red heart) than I do Vietnamese. The yellow star represents how people see me similarly to how I feel and who I am. The green and blue arrow represents the languages I can understand when I listen to people speak, I can understand Vietnamese and English, however I am only fluent in English and my Vietnamese is broken and not strong enough to have a long conversation.

Our response

Tham is Vietnamese by descent but 'feels more Australian than Vietnamese'. She can understand and speak 'broken' Vietnamese, but insists she feels 'little connection' to her Vietnamese roots. Yet her silhouette is almost entirely coloured in pink: the colour she chose to represent her Vietnamese heritage.

Classroom application

Visual – The silhouette initially points to the participant's close connection to her heritage language and culture. The entire body is coloured pink (Vietnamese) and the face is covered by the yellow star of the national flag. Yet, the participant suggests that she feels far more Australian, as symbolised by the red heart. The dissonance related to dual languages and cultural identity is a valuable topic for students to explore.

PMI – You see yourself as Australian first, with English being the language you speak most of the time. Does this define who you are? Conduct a PMI to explore this statement.

C&S – What are the advantages of keeping your heritage language and culture 'alive'? How will this benefit you in your future life?

APC – Consider different ways to improve your heritage language skills outside the home? (E.g. Friendships, social and community activities, sport, travel, technology/media).

Keywords: Vietnamese, identity

Figure 42. Samantha is a 20-year old female student who speaks Greek and English at home, and learned Italian in high school.

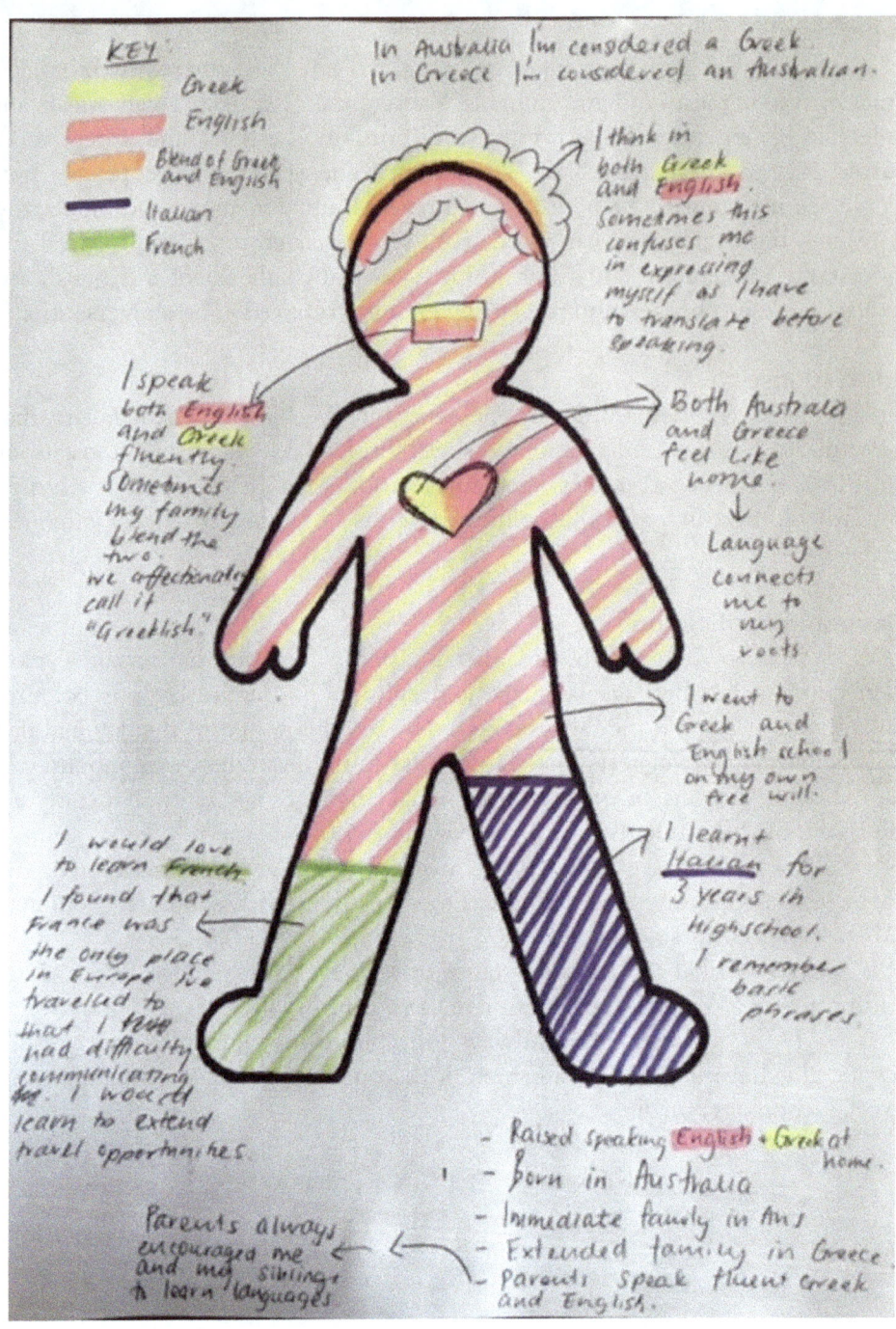

Samantha is a 20-year old female student who speaks Greek and English at home, and learned Italian in high school.

In her words

I think in both Greek and English and can speak both fluently (Fig. 42). Sometimes this confuses me in expressing myself as I have to translate before speaking. I chose yellow to represent Greek and pink to represent English. I went to Greek and English school. In Australia, I am considered a Greek; in Greece, I am considered an Australian. Italian is coloured in a smaller section as I have only spent 3 years learning it and I don't speak it very often. Language overall connects me to my roots and to my ancestors and I am very fortunate to have been presented with the resources and opportunities to learn additional languages. I am proud to be a third-generation Greek who is fluent in Greek.

Our response

Samantha is a third-generation Greek, yet her links to her Greek heritage are strong and nurtured by her parents. She went to a bilingual Greek-English school and is one of a few who are academically competent in heritage and English languages. Both her Greek and English/Australian selves blend effortlessly in her being. Similarly, in their communication her family switches effortlessly between languages in what they 'affectionately call "Greeklish"'. Yet while she strongly identifies with her Greek and Australian/English selves, she laconically states, 'In Australia I'm considered a Greek; In Greece, I am considered an Australian'.

Classroom application

Visual – Pink and yellow colours combine in lively candy cane stripes to suggest the harmonious blend between the Greek and English languages in the participant's life. However, this close connection also suggests a point where the identity of the participant might become blurred. She notes how her national identity shifts according to how others see her. This could be an interesting classroom discussion to pursue.

CAF (Related series of questions)
– How do you define your identity? Is there such a thing as a single identity? Do you see yourself differently in different situations? How strongly does this relate to your heritage language and culture?
– If you were to advise anyone on the best ways to maintain their heritage language and culture, what would you suggest?

OPV – How accepting is the wider Australian community of different languages and cultures? Try to provide some examples based on your own experience.

Keywords: Greek, Italian, community language school

Figure 43. Hasna is a 21-year old female student who speaks Tamil and English at home.

Hasna is a 21-year old female student who speaks Tamil and English at home.

In her words

I've coloured in my silhouette (Fig. 43) equally into two distinctive sections to represent how both the languages have had an equal impact in shaping my identity: Tamil (green) and English (orange). English is the language I had to learn after I migrated to Australia as a child. My native language is well integrated in to my life with my family, culture and tradition. After migrating to Australia, English is also a very crucial aspect of my life as it has helped me gain good education and make friends with others from different cultural backgrounds. It has helped me mingle with people in this multicultural society. I have used the English language to my advantage throughout school, university and now the workplace too, hence why I've coloured in that section across my brain (representing knowledge). Tamil shapes my identity and plays a crucial part in strengthening some of the most valuable relationships I have with my family and my country Sri Lanka. This is why I've coloured in that part close my heart, being my emotional connection to my language, culture and country.

Our response

Hasna seems comfortable about the balance between English which has advantaged her educationally, socially and professionally, as well as helping her to integrate in multicultural Australian life. When she says that she will try her hardest to keep in touch with her native language, Tamil, symbolised by a red heart, this seems to indicate that in spite of the advantages she identifies in speaking English, it is essential to maintain the language skills and emotional connection to her culture and country of origin. (She might fear the loss of this, but this can only be implied indirectly).

Classroom application

Visual – The silhouette is striking in that it draws the eye directly to the symbol of the brain, representing the advantages of learning English, and the heart, being the emotional connection to the participant's heritage language.

CAF – Think of all the things you love about your heritage language. List these, then think about what defines your identity in a multicultural world.

APC – Besides speaking your heritage language at home, can you think of other ways to keep your language and culture alive in your multicultural world? (e.g. friendships, community, social, cultural activities, and travel).

AGO – What opportunities can you envisage in the future which will make use of your heritage language, or knowledge of other languages, besides English?

Keywords: Tamil, identity, heritage, migration

Figure 44. Shanu is a 20-year old female student who speaks Hindi and English at home, learned Italian in school, learned Japanese, Spanish and Turkish from friends and TV.

Shanu is a 20-year old female student who speaks Hindi and English at home, learned Italian in school, learned Japanese, Spanish and Turkish from friends and TV.

In her words

My language portrait silhouette depicts the integration of two languages, English and Hindi (Fig. 44). I was born in Australia and therefore I was taught to speak English at a young age. It became my first language. However, my heritage language is Hindi. My grandparents lived with me until late primary, and to be able to communicate with them I was also taught Hindi. As a result, I speak it quite fluently. I cannot read Hindi or write it. Hindi was not only used to communicate to my grandparents and other family members but was also used to keep the connection with my heritage. I have Turkish neighbours, and over the years I have learnt to pick up some Turkish words and their meanings when listening to them having conversations in their language.

Our response

Shanu asserts that English is her first language as she was born in Australia and had a wide circle of people with whom she could converse in English. It was also the language of her school. At the same time, because her grandparents lived with them in her early years, Shanu was taught Hindi in order to be able to communicate with them. This is her heritage language, but Shanu only uses it to speak with her family. As such, she never learnt to read nor write in Hindi and her language development in Hindi has not progressed beyond what she has learnt from speaking with her family.

Classroom application

Visual – The drawing in the silhouette is accompanied by detailed written explanations. The opportunity to draw this silhouette seems to have released a stream of ideas which the participant has expressed as a narrative relating to her language and cultural history. Some students might find it a useful example to express ideas in a similar format.

C&S – Consider this scenario:
Nina enjoys speaking to her family, especially grandparents in her heritage language _____. She speaks fluently, but feels concerned that she has never learnt to read or write her home language without a stronger grammatical foundation. Use a C&S to predict the outcome of this in the future.

APC – How can competence in heritage and other languages assist you in learning new languages more easily? Suggest reasons why (e.g. relate to listening, speaking, vocabulary and thinking).

Keywords: Hindi, Italian, Japanese, Spanish, Turkish, heritage, grandparents

Figure 45. Cherry is a 23-year old female student who speaks English and Vietnamese at home.

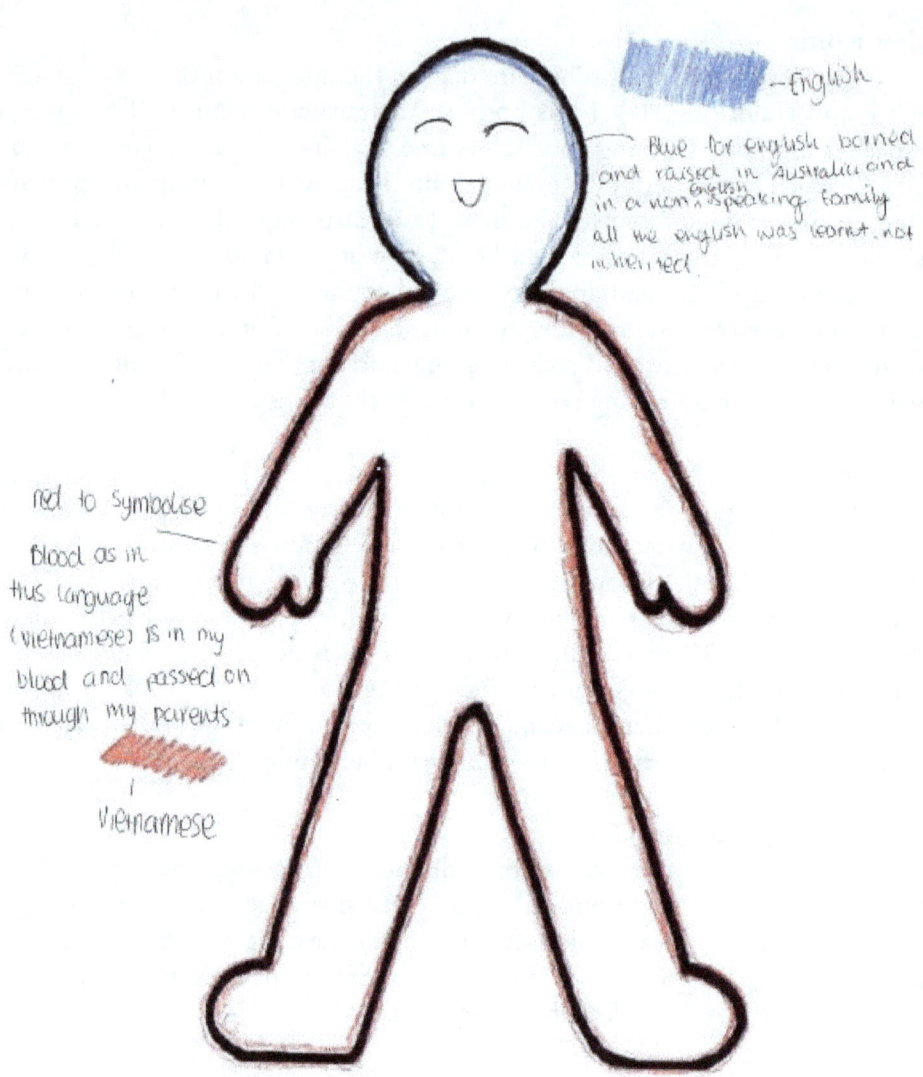

Cherry is a 23-year old female student who speaks English and Vietnamese at home.

In her words
The red outlining most of the body symbolises how my parents have given me Vietnamese blood (Fig. 45). The Vietnamese blood that courses throughout my body is my identity and who I am as a person. I speak and fully understand Vietnamese. I have chosen to colour my head in blue for English. I have also chosen to only colour my head blue because even though my ethnicity is Vietnamese, and I present visually as a full Vietnamese female, I speak and write in English and also think in English. I am more fluent in English. Growing up in a rather traditional Vietnamese home, I was unable to learn English from my parents. All my English was learnt, not inherited.

Our response
Cherry is conscious of the fact that she 'visually' presents as Vietnamese. She has 'Vietnamese blood' and this is her identity. Be that as it may, Cherry considers English to be her first language of competency. Vietnamese is confined to her home. There is also an interesting concept of language as an inheritance, which may or may not be welcomed by the students.

Classroom application
Visual – The blue outline around head indicates the importance of speaking, writing and thinking in English, whereas the blood red outline symbolises the participant's Vietnamese ethnicity and identity. There is a clear demarcation between her sense of traditional belonging versus the necessity to participate successfully in the outside world, (the considerable amount of effort to master English without the assistance of her parents). This might be a familiar experience for many students to discuss.

PMI – *Heritage languages, or learning new languages, should take second place to learning to speak and write in English at an advanced level.* Discuss the pros and cons of this statement using a PMI.

C&S – Read the following scenario:
A Chinese student has always communicated with his parents and grandparents in his heritage language. He hardly ever uses his home language outside of his home, preferring to speak in English. Consider the consequences of this now and for the future.

AGO – How do you define who you are and how you see yourself in the world around you?

APC – What are the different ways you can maintain your heritage language outside of your home? (E.g. Social and community activities, hobbies)

Keywords: Vietnamese, identity

Figure 46. Nafiye is a 21-year old female student who speaks Macedonian at home.

Nafiye is a 21-year old female student who speaks Macedonian at home.

In her words

I decided to colour in my silhouette half representing the colours of the Australian flag and half representing the colours of the Macedonian flag (Fig. 46). I coloured in my language portrait silhouette in such a way because I am fluent in both languages. I have lived half my life in Macedonia and half of my life in Australia so attending both English and Macedonian schools really helped me learn the languages more proficiently. I usually speak Macedonian at home with my parents because they are only fluent in Macedonian and speak English as their second language. However, at university, work and almost everywhere else outside of school I tend to speak the English language. I am fortunate enough however to have also attended Macedonian school here in Sydney or also known as community languages or Saturday school. That also helped me maintain my Macedonian language outside of the household and I also regularly speak it without exception when I go overseas to Macedonia with my family and friends. Thus, my language portrait silhouette represents just that, my split love for both languages.

Our response

The importance of attending community language schools during weekends and after school hours may not have been emphasised by many parents. However, many participants view the community language schools as opportunities to connect with their heritage culture beyond their own families. Many people tell of tales of these childhood learning experiences.

Classroom application

Visual – The body is coloured from head to toe, half in the Australian flag and half in the colours of the Macedonian flag. This clearly symbolises the harmonious balance between both languages and cultures in the participant's life. Teachers could use this silhouette as a discussion point for students: How easy or difficult is it to move between heritage and mainstream languages?

CAF – If you were to advise anyone on the best ways to maintain their heritage language, what would you say? Try to consider what you might have left out.

C&S – What careers have you thought about for the future? Why would a strong foundation in your heritage and/or other languages be an advantage to you? Use a C&S to establish the relevance of this connection.
– What will be the consequences of keeping your heritage language 'alive'?

OPV – How will knowledge of different languages and cultures help you understand other points of view.

Keywords: Macedonian, community language school, heritage, identity

Figure 47. Andrew is a 27-year old male student who speaks Lebanese Arabic at home, learned French while on holiday, and Punjabi from friends.

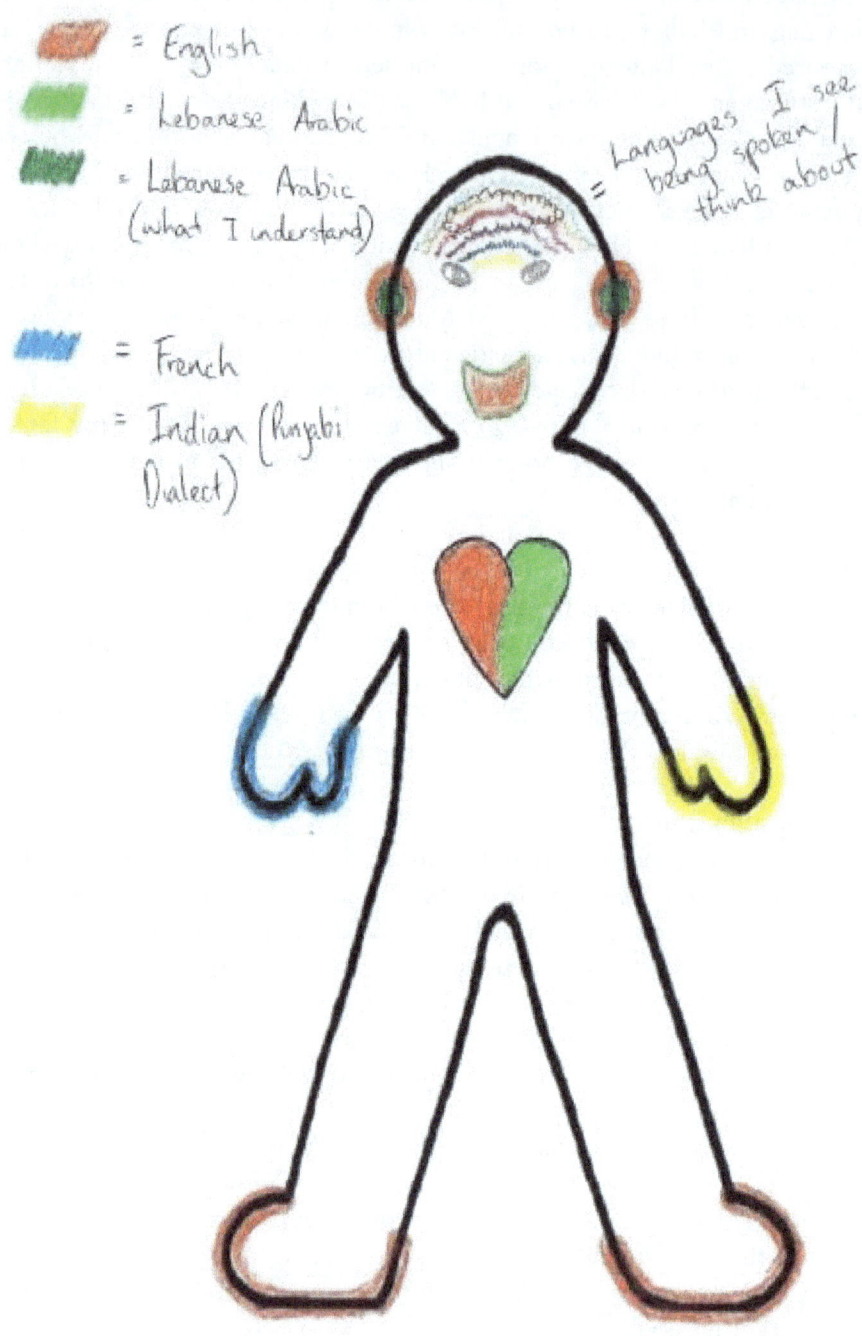

Andrew is a 27-year old male student who speaks Lebanese Arabic at home, learned French while on holiday, and Punjabi from friends.

In his words

English and Lebanese Arabic are the two languages I have grown up with in my life and what I am strongly connected to (Fig. 47). The Lebanese is from both of my parents and makes up 50% of what is spoken at home, the English is the other half of what is spoken at home. English is what I use more often in everyday life (outside of home). The light green depicts how I use Lebanese in sentences as a sentence may include both English and Lebanese words (briefly). The darker green for the ears is the Lebanese Arabic I can understand but struggle to repeat when trying to use it in conversation. The blue and yellow hands are languages I have briefly picked up from going overseas and from friends (French and Indian), I do not excel in these languages but can speak the necessary words to get me by. Finally, the top of my head shows my brain connected to my eyes by the languages I see in the world and are thought about with my brain as to what is being said by those using the languages.

Our response

Andrew has a strong awareness of the gap between his competencies in listening (stronger) and speaking (weaker). This can be a good way to encourage self-assessment and open a discussion with students to consider strategies to enhance learning.

Classroom application

Visual – The feet of the silhouette are symbolically grounded in English. The head though, suggests the participant's immersion in several languages, as indicated in the bands of colours beneath his deeper connection to his heritage language and English. Teachers, and even the students themselves, might be surprised by the extent of their multilingual skills. These can be shared and celebrated in the classroom.

PMI – *Language is best learnt the traditional way, through grammar, spelling rules and practice in the classroom.* Conduct a PMI on this statement.

APC – What are some of the alternative ways of learning languages outside of formal classroom learning? (E.g. Family, friends, community activities, involvement in the arts, sport and media/technology).
– How can your knowledge of your heritage and other languages advance your skills and ability to learn new languages?

Keywords: Arabic, French, Punjabi, friends, heritage, family

Figure 48. Hamayoon is a 22-year old male student who speaks Dari and Farsi at home.

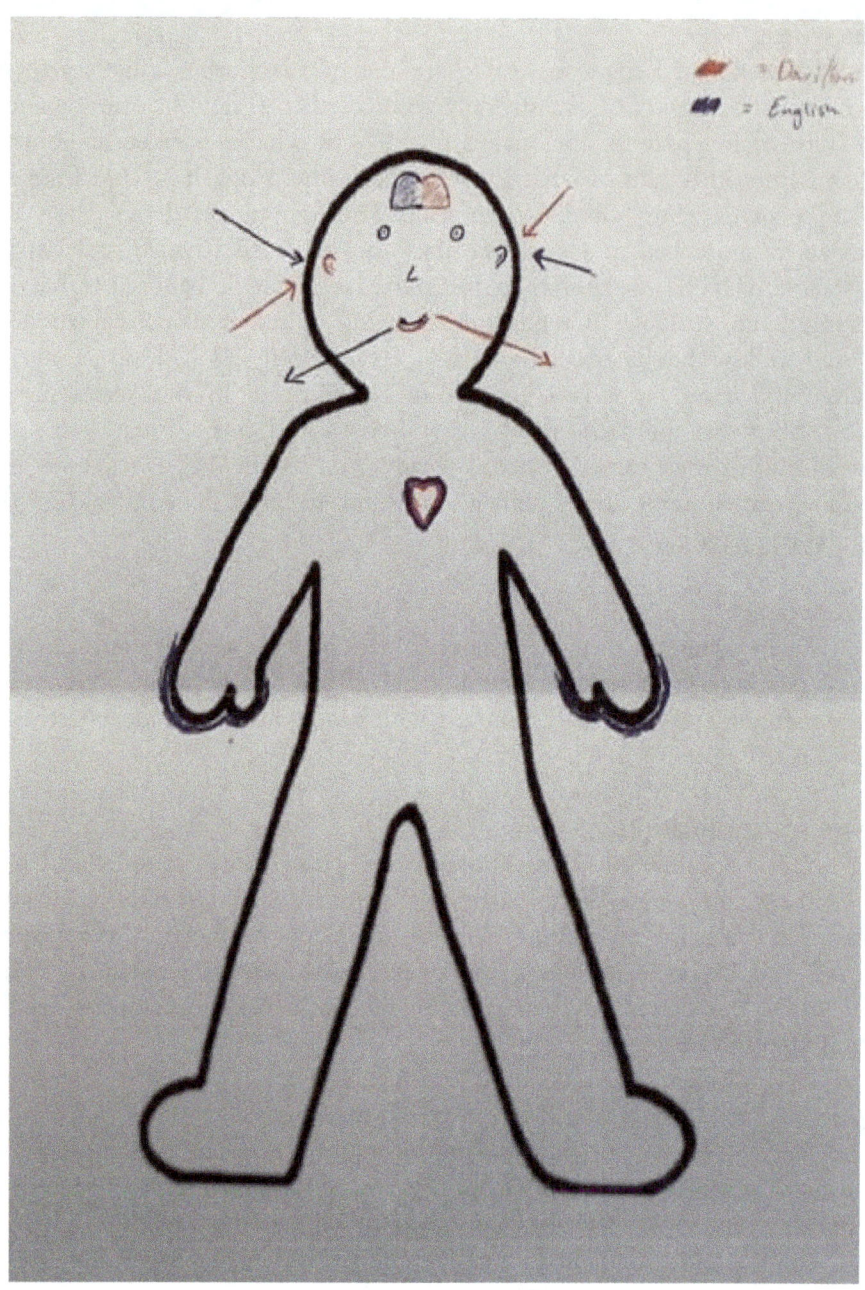

Hamayoon is a 22-year old male student who speaks Dari and Farsi at home.

In his words

My silhouette shows how I perceive and make meaning of the world (Fig. 48). It addresses how I use my five senses and meaning I gain from these senses in regards to the language and/or culture. I use more English than Dari, however, I am still immersed in the language by speaking Dari at home. My inner thoughts and desires are directly linked with my upbringing and culture, as well as the contemporary society. So, a combination of both is created - as seen in the heart and mind of my silhouette.

Our response

Hamayoon makes an interesting observation that he uses English (with his hands), but his mind and heart is shared with Dari and Farsi.

Classroom application

Visual – The arrows around the head of the figure point to the ears and mouth indicating equal representation between the participant's heritage language and use of English. The heart symbolising his deep connection to his upbringing and culture, while the hands represent his connection to the mainstream world. This recognition of the division between emotional and practical selves could be a talking point which heritage language learners can identify with.

CAF – Consider how the five senses (sight, hearing, taste, touch and smell) can be used to promote language learning. Separate each sense and list some examples.

AGO – What is identity? Does this mean different things in different contexts? How do you then define who you are?

OPV – How can an individual's knowledge of their own heritage language and culture affect their worldview and understanding of others?

Keywords: Dari, Farsi, emotion

Figure 49. Stella is a 21-year old female student who speaks English and Spanish at home.

Stella is a 21-year old female student who speaks English and Spanish at home.

In her words

The cloud of blue that crowns my head is the hazy presence of Spanish (blue) in my life (Fig. 49). It enters my mind at times, and there is an intense degree of familiarity, yet perceivable distance. My entire experience with Spanish is framed by English (burgundy), hence the frame around the silhouette. In many situations, I find my understanding of English from grammatical perspectives hinders my understanding of Spanish. This creates a wall around my brain, which is created by my English education, and my reduced confidence to embarrass myself for the purpose of exploring a new language that lies just out of reach.

Our response

Stella highlights a different mindset is needed when learning a new language, and the thrills of being changed in one's mannerism by learning a new language. It is important to understand that by learning a new language, we are not simply learning to translate, but to view the differences in the language systems.

Classroom application

Visual – The head of the figure appears to be imprisoned by walls which represent the possible interference which English has imposed on learning new languages. The free-form representation of Spanish as a cloud around the head suggests its lack of tangibility as the participant's heritage language. This contrast highlights the interference which knowledge of one language can impose on another, a useful discussion in the classroom.

CAF – If you wish to advise anyone on the value of learning their heritage language from an early age, what would you say based on your own experience?

AGO – Identify the avenues which generate the most possibilities of keeping your heritage language 'alive.'
– How can learning a new language influence your life and future? Discuss.

FIP – When you decide to learn a new language what are the most important factors to take into account? (E.g. Time, commitment, formal learning such as grammar and vocabulary, practice, etc.). How will these practices increase the likelihood of success and more confidence in language mastery?

Keywords: Spanish, challenge

Figure 50. Mafalda is a 21-year old female student who speaks English and Italian at home, and learned Spanish and German from travels and friends.

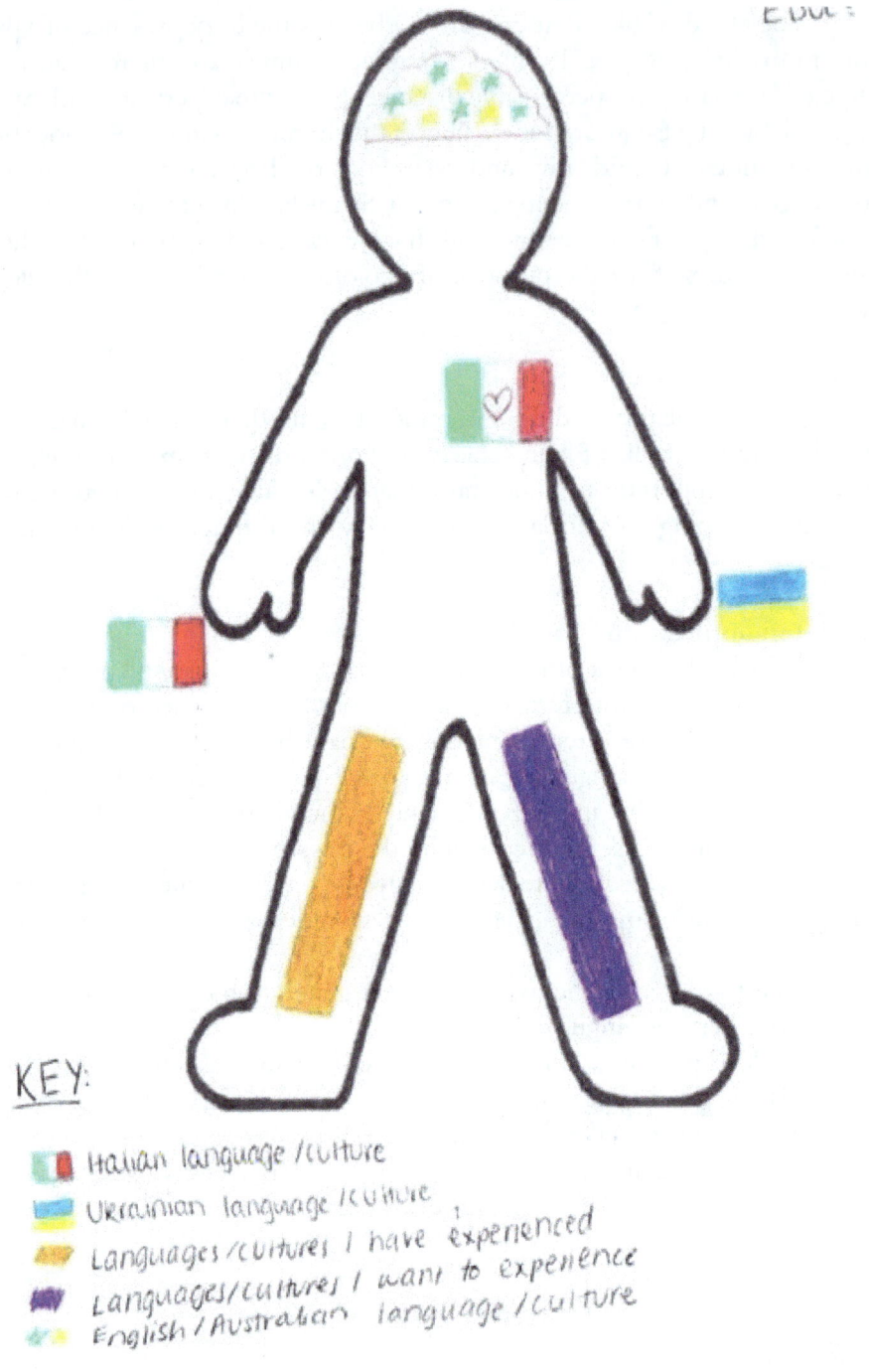

Mafalda is a 21-year old female student who speaks English and Italian at home, and learned Spanish and German from travels and friends.

In her words

In my language portrait silhouette (Fig. 50) I used (1) green, white and red to represent the Italian flag and culture; (2) blue and yellow to represent the Ukrainian flag and culture; and (3) green and yellow stars to represent English Australian language and culture. Italian is positioned in the heart as I wish I could speak fluent Italian to better communicate and connect with my maternal grandparents, and Ukrainian with my father's side of the family. I drew the Italian and Ukrainian flag at the end of each hand to represent my grasp to learn the language of my heritage.

Our response

Wanting to communicate with grandparents is frequently mentioned by community language learners as a motivation to learn, and unfortunately, as a regret mentioned by many of these young adults, as well.

Classroom application

Visual – Simple vibrant colours highlight the participant's two heritage language national flags. The Italian flag is placed central to the figure, incorporating the symbol of a heart. The layout of this silhouette clearly shows the participant's language diversity and identity. A simple combination of colour and symbolism provides a useful catalyst for students to recognise the importance of heritage language, culture and their connections to family.

CAF – Consider all the things you love most about your heritage language and culture. List these, then discuss what your culture means to you, anything you feel strongly about and what you might have left out of this picture (e.g. Extended family connections and language loss).
– If you wish to advise anyone on the value of maintaining their heritage language and culture, what would you say? (Can adapt this to learning a new language, as well).

AGO - Identify the avenues which generate the most possibilities of keeping your heritage language 'alive.' (This can include cultural, as well as language connections, e.g. time spent with grandparents - songs, cooking, memories, etc.).

Keywords: Italian, Spanish, German, travel

Figure 51. Emilia is a 21-year old female student who speaks English and Bulgarian at home and learned French.

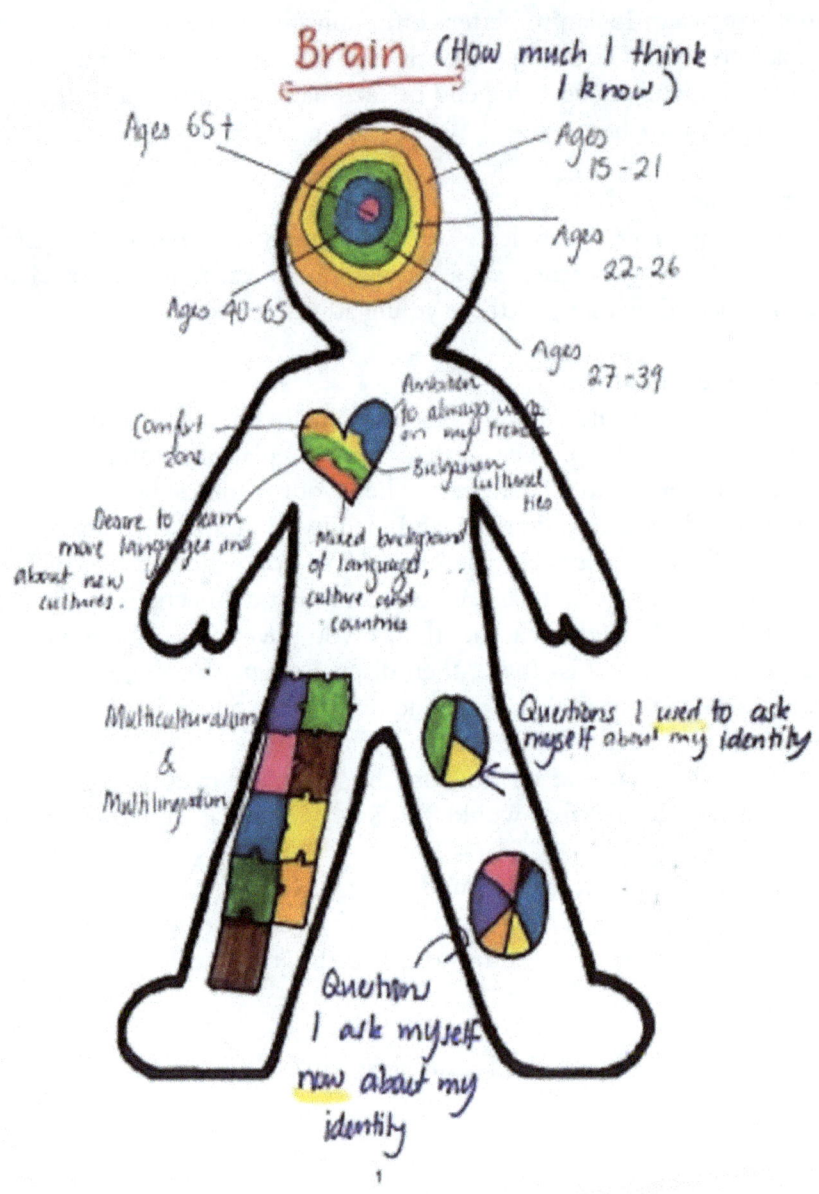

Emilia is a 21-year old female student who speaks English and Bulgarian at home and learned French.

In her words
The vibrant colours, patterns and swirls all accord to my knowledge of languages, the languages I feel determine my culture and identity, and the feelings associated with my role in society (Fig. 51). I drew a large circle descending into smaller ones, labelling it with age groups, on my 'head'. This visual representation highlights how much I think I know at a particular age. The younger I was, the more I thought I knew, and as I grow older I am beginning to realise how little I know. The puzzles and pie charts drawn on my legs symbolise growth.

Our response
Emilia projects the extent of her knowledge as she develops, and humbly thinks as she gets older that she will come to understand the limit of her knowledge of language. This prompts her to want to know more.

Classroom application
Visual – It is a complex idea to represent the development of language proficiency over time. The drawings include age ranges, pie charts and puzzles to chart a meaningful journey towards multilingualism and establishing the participant's identity at the present time. The silhouette has provided a meaningful space to reflect on this process.

C&S – Language can define cultural identity and your place in society now, although this might change in the future. Do a C&S to explore this statement.

AGO – What is identity? How do you define who you are and how does this change over time?
– What goals do you set for yourself in the future?
– How many of your AGO's are influenced by your heritage language, acquisition of other languages and cultures?

Keywords: Bulgarian, French, identity

Figure 52. Judy is a 21-year old female student who speaks English and Vietnamese at home, and learned Japanese at school.

Judy is a 21-year old female student who speaks English and Vietnamese at home, and learned Japanese at school.

In her words

I identify as a Vietnamese Australian, and this is shown in the background of my language portrait silhouette: half a Vietnamese flag and half an Australian flag (Fig. 52). I am wearing the traditional Vietnamese costume (ao dai) on one side and the typical Australian attire on the other. I speak both Vietnamese and English fluently and I am grateful that I had the opportunity to have had a rich language exposure at a young age. There is also a tiny Japanese flag on the bottom, which represents the basic Japanese culture and language knowledge that I learned in high school.

Our response

Judy is clear that both Vietnamese and Australian cultures have made her the person who she is, and her early exposure to Vietnamese encouraged her to do well later in high school Japanese class.

Classroom application

Visual – The participant has transformed the silhouette into a work of art. Although she acknowledges her identity as half Vietnamese and half Australian, the Vietnamese flag dominates overall. This is arranged like a crown around her head suggesting a deeper emotional connection to her heritage language. Artistically creative students might enjoy the freedom to express their ideas in more elaborate detail in the silhouette.

PMI – *A new language can be learnt in 100 hours.* Conduct a PMI to explore the pros and cons of this statement.

CAF – If you were to advise anyone on the value of maintaining their heritage language, what would you say, based on your own experience?
– Think of all the things you love most about your heritage language and culture, and compare to the English language and Australian culture. List these in two columns, then think which factors combine to define your identity.

Keywords: Vietnamese, Japanese, identity

Figure 53. Alexis is a 20-year old female student who learned some Polish through a friend and family.

Alexis is a 20-year old female student who learned some Polish through a friend and family.

In her words

I was born in Australia and the only language I know, understand and speak is English, thus it is written through my whole body and surrounds me (Fig. 53). I wrote Polish in the hands and feet of my silhouette due to my family heritage. My great grandmother and my grandmother were both born in Poland and migrated to Australia many years ago. My great grandmother speaks English most of the time but likes to use her heritage language in some circumstance. My great grandmother rarely speaks Polish in my presence, so I don't understand much at all. My friend is Polish and lives in Poland. She has taught me to say a few different words and phrases, especially when I went and stayed with her. This is a small connection but still means something to me as it is part of my family heritage and is a major aspect of my friend's life.

Our response

Students who are monolingual, with some limited exposure to other languages, often indicate that they feel disadvantaged compared to bi/multilingual students. Students would not be in this position if schools provided more opportunities and encouragement to learn a foreign language. The participant's 'loss' of learning a second language is compounded by the disappointment that her heritage language has been denied her and not passed on through her family.

Classroom application

Visual – The silhouette is crammed with large printed writing which almost seem to prop it up. This exaggerates the participant's monolingualism and feelings of disappointment about her lack of second language acquisition. Students can be encouraged to use a variety of lettering to effectively convey different emotions and ideas in their silhouettes.

CAF – What factors should you consider when learning a new language? (E.g. time commitment, future career, love of a specific language or culture). List your main ideas for discussion, then try to think of any others you might have left out.

– What are some of the ways to encourage maintenance of your heritage language/other language skills besides learning in the classroom? (E.g. connections to family, friends, community, music, art, drama, literature, sport, technology/media).

AGO – What reasons would you give to others to learn a new language?

Keywords: Polish, friends

Figure 54. Pompiliu is a 24-year old male student who speaks Romanian at home, and learned English in school and Spanish from his partner's family.

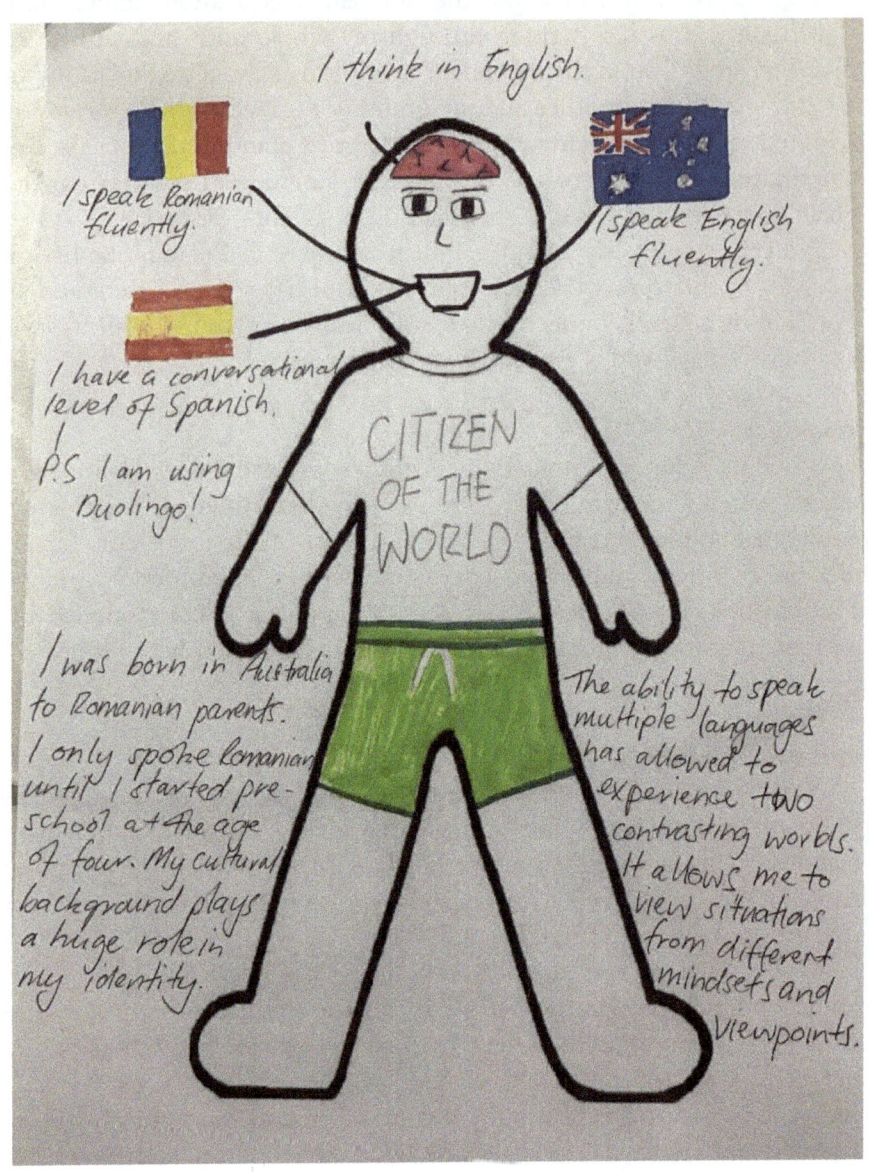

Pompiliu is a 24-year old male student who speaks Romanian at home, and learned English in school and Spanish from his partner's family.

In his words

I chose to colour my silhouette in this way because I feel like my life has been split into two worlds (Fig. 54). I grew up until the age of 4 only speaking Romanian, and only picked up English at the start of pre-school. Spanish is also a very big component as many close family friends are of Spanish-speaking background, and I developed a conversational level of Spanish. It also really helps that Romanian and Spanish are Latin-based languages, so many of the words are very similar. I am very proud of my multilingualism, and it is a big part of who I am.

Our response

Speaking more than one language is not just an 'ability', it partly makes us who we are! Bi/multilingual research suggests that some people use different languages to express their emotions, e.g. expressing closeness through one's heritage language only, or using a particular language to express anger.

Classroom application

Visual – The written explanations and visual symbolism in the participant's silhouette suggests his ease and confident attitude about the way he sees himself as a 'citizen of the world.' This clearly relates to his proficiency in multiple languages. In older students, deeper written reflection often complements the visual representation of ideas in the drawings.

AGO – What is identity? How do you define yourself?

APC – How can the acquisition of bi/multilingual skills change your life? Consider opportunities it creates now and possibilities for the future.

OPV – Are individuals who are bi/multilingual likely to see other points of view more clearly? Discuss in relation to your own language diversity and the experiences you have had.

Keywords: Romanian, Spanish, friends

Figure 55. Maggie is a 32-year old female student who speaks Cantonese and English at home.

Maggie is a 32-year old female student who speaks Cantonese and English at home.

In her words

The languages I speak fluently are Cantonese and English but I predominately speak English (Fig. 55). I find speaking Cantonese in public a little uncomfortable. Subconsciously I find it rude speaking Cantonese in an Anglo-Saxon dominated culture. Consequently, I coloured a black bubble around me, to act as a barrier. I keep most of my Chinese roots within me and tend to only use it when my parents are around. I hope society can see the benefits of my native tongue. I strongly feel my Cantonese and my culture can be of a resource for everyone. Thus, I have used many colours around the barrier to show this.

Our response

Many bi/multilinguals share this point: it is 'rude' to speak a language other than English in public. When, as a country, we are ready to accept that language and cultural diversity is as common as the air we breathe, we cannot truly claim to be a 'multicultural' country.

Classroom application

Visual – The participant is strongly aware of cultural norms in the dominant culture. This inhibits her use of her heritage language in public and clouds her identity, shown by the black bubble which surrounds the figure. The silhouette can act as a powerful voice to express repressed views on how heritage language learners might see themselves within Australian society.

AGO – What is identity? How do you define who you are?

APC – What language choices do you make when you are with your close and extended family, your friends or out in the wider community? How does this affect your life and what might you change?

OPV – Do you find the wider Australian community is accepting of language and cultural diversity? Can you think of some examples when this might or might not be the case?

Keywords: Cantonese, family

Figure 56. Frank is a 23-year old male student who speaks English and Arabic at home, and learned French in school.

Frank is a 23-year old male student who speaks English and Arabic at home, and learned French in school.

In his words

I was brought up in an English-speaking household, yet my background is Arabic Lebanese (Fig. 56). The Lebanese flag is the second largest as I am heavily influenced by Lebanese culture in both my household, and when visiting, or going to events with extended family and friends. I learnt French in high school. I only learnt French for about three years. However, in this time I learned more French than I know Arabic, even though I've been brought up around several relatives that can either only speak Arabic, or predominantly do so.

Our response

Frank acknowledges the loss of his heritage language, even as he expresses the positive gain of learning a foreign language through formal school learning. Regret for lack of proficiency and fluency in home languages is not an uncommon theme among students when they are immersed in the mainstream community, with the dominant language being English.

Classroom application

Visual – Students are not always given the opportunity to express the dissonance they experience at the potential loss of their heritage languages. The silhouette captures this in the bold representation of the Australian and French flags covering the entire body, with the shrunken central image of the Lebanese flag symbolised as the mouth.

CAF – Consider the factors which interfere with the maintenance of your heritage language. List a few of the most difficult ones, then discuss possible plans to solve these problems constructively.

C&S: What will be the consequences of either:
a) Keeping your heritage language 'alive,' or,
b) Losing your heritage language.

APC – Identify the avenues which generate the best possibilities for you to keep your heritage language skills actively used and advanced to a higher level. (E.g. at home, in school/ community language schools, in social and cultural activities in the community, via multimedia and technology, language apps, etc.).

Keywords: Arabic, French, family, school

Figure 57. Eliza is a 22-year old female student who speaks English and Italian at home, and learned Italian, French and Japanese in school.

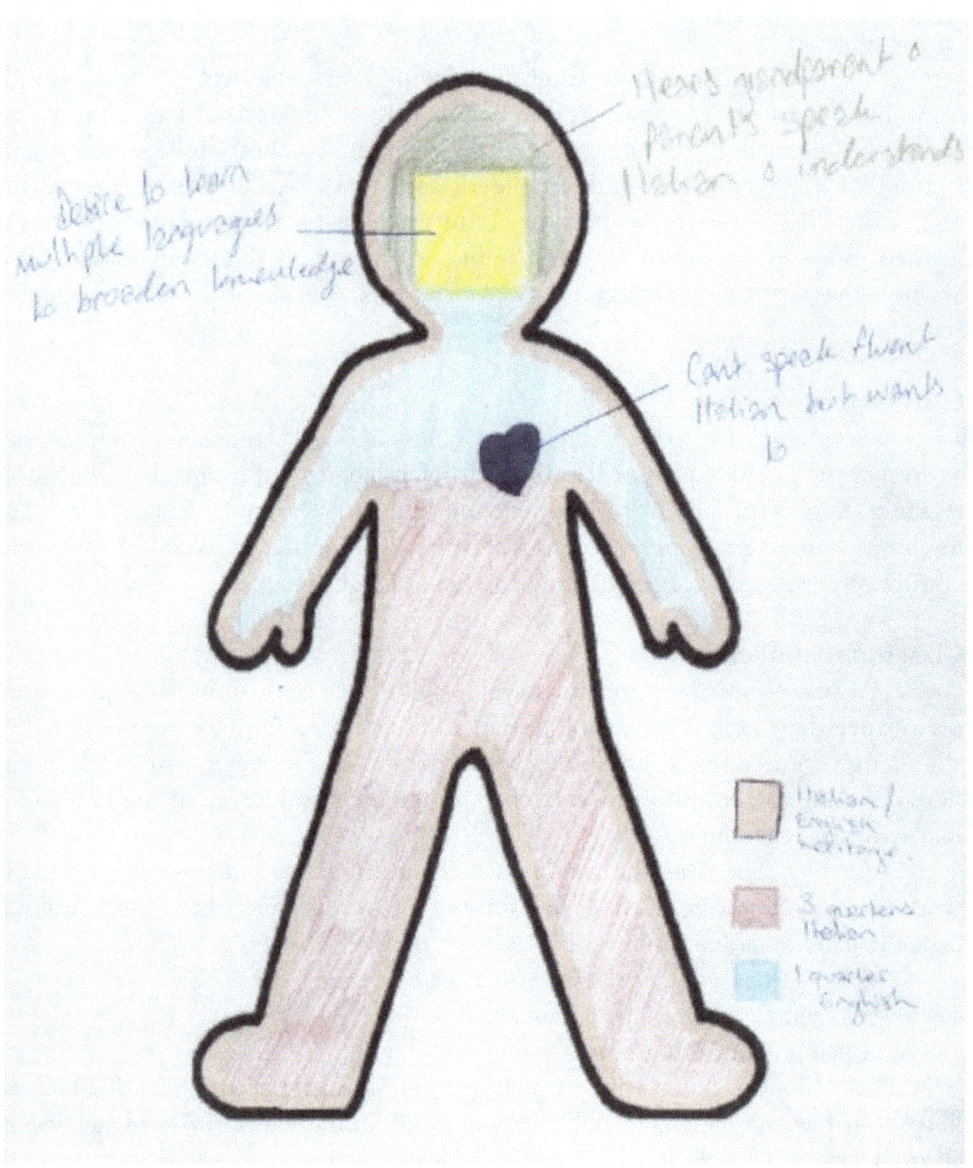

Eliza is a 22-year old female student who speaks English and Italian at home, and learned Italian, French and Japanese in school.

In her words

I chose red and blue (Fig. 57) because they contrast each other while the orange highlighter around the edge represents what everybody sees first (my physical appearance). The green was to represent what I hear and think while the yellow is what I observe and learn in everyday life. While I like to discover different languages through listening and reading, I find it hard to reproduce it verbally through fear of being criticised or the possibility of saying the wrong thing.

Our response

Many (community) language learners also share this similar tale: the fear of being criticized when they cannot produce the language correctly. What can teachers/families do to support a positive environment for language learning?

Classroom application

Visual – The silhouette is completely shaded in colours to represent the diversity of languages spoken. It is the written explanation which reveals the participant's anxiety and inhibitions about using her heritage language, Italian. The silhouette acts as a means to express emotions and contemplate positive future goals to redress loss of language proficiency. It can act as a catalyst and future motivating force.

PMI – *Language fluency cannot be complete without formal grammar, reading and writing instruction.* Conduct a PMI to examine this statement.

CAF – What are the different ways in which you can practice speaking your heritage language or other languages outside the classroom? List these, then consider other avenues which might be less obvious.

CAF or FIP – When you decide to learn a new language what are the most important things to take into account? (E.g. time, commitment, availability of formal learning opportunities, love of language, etc.).

Keywords: Italian, French, Japanese, family, school

Figure 58. Daniel is a 22-year old male student who speaks German at home, and learned English, Russian and Nepali.

Daniel is a 22-year old male student who speaks German at home, and learned English, Russian and Nepali.

In his words

English dominates a large part of my personality and identity, having lived in Australia since 1999 (Fig. 58). Next is German, the language of family. Physically my voice has often been described as an angry German drill sergeant by the people I play sports with. My Nepali side comes from my travels in Nepal and the love I have of their spices as well as my unhurried nature (a constant battle with my German side). Finally, after having been immersed in the Russian culture from my previous relationship, I adopted what has been called my "Russian stare" – people find I tend to bore holes straight through them.

Our response

As with many others, Daniel picked up two new languages and cultures from his travel and personal relationships. Language learning can happen anytime when we are open to it.

Classroom application

Visual – Although the participant cites English and German as central to his daily life, he shades Russian and Nepali in equal parts in the head of the silhouette. A portion of one hand (Russian) and one foot (German) indicate their added significance in his life. Each body section of the silhouette lends itself to multicultural expression of identity.

CAF – Think about all the things you love or admire about the languages you speak and their related cultures. List these. How does this influence and define who you are?

– Does language acquisition and cultural knowledge only relate to home and school environments? Consider other possible ways in which you can learn languages and experience different cultures.

OPV – Discuss how knowledge of different languages can help you understand other people's views on life? Think of examples from your own experience.

Keywords: German, Russian, Nepali, travel, school

Figure 59. Branca is a 21-year old female student who speaks Portuguese and Spanish at home, and learned French in school.

Branca is a 21-year old female student who speaks Portuguese and Spanish at home, and learned French in school.

In her words

Blue (English) outlines the figures and the mouth because that is my dominant language (Fig. 59). Portuguese is the language of my culture, and is in pink, a passionate colour. Pink has been used only for the eyes and ears because it is a language I can understand and recognise but not speak. Pink flowers lie on top of the blue grass as from my understanding of English I hope to 'grow' fluency in Portuguese. Spanish is in yellow, a warm colour I associate with my family in South America. Yellow flowers stem from the pink as my knowledge of Portuguese will assist my understanding of Spanish.

Our response

Branca makes connections between different languages, and explains how knowing one language may help her to learn another. She is also unusual in giving a 'background' and adding flowers to the drawing! Often, participants tend to only represent a figure without any background.

Classroom application

Visual – The participant seems to prefer more delicate forms of expressions, rather than bold colours. The background to the silhouette is coloured a light shade of blue, which together with the darker blue outline symbolises English as her dominant language. Teachers can gain useful insight about individual student's interpretations of heritage languages, such as the unusual dual flower heads and encircled heart.

CAF – If you were to advise anyone of the value of maintaining their heritage languages, what would you say?

C&S – How can learning and understanding one language make it easier to learn and speak other languages in the future?

OPV – Discuss how knowledge of different languages can help you to understand other people's views on life? Think of examples from your own experience.

Keywords: Portuguese, Spanish, French, family

Figure 60. Rita is a 24-year old female student who speaks Maltese and Swahili at home, and learned Japanese and Tagalog.

Rita is a 24-year old female student who speaks Maltese and Swahili at home, and learned Japanese and Tagalog.

In her words

The hair represents my family's language heritage and roots: South African and Maltese (Fig. 60). The heart in the centre represents what I identify myself as in terms of nationality but all other aspects make up my culture. My family comes from both Malta and South Africa, yet we also identify as Australian. I hear English in different dialects and accents and it all makes up a part of me. The other languages floating around my body represent the languages I want to learn. The two languages on my arms are the languages that I continue to learn and to one day hopefully become fluent in.

Our response

It is unusual that Rita mentioned English in various forms and dialects. In Australia, English tends to be treated as a more singular term, Australian English. In reality, multilingual and multicultural Australian speak Englishes.

Classroom application

Visual – Added bodily features external to the silhouette, such as the flowing hair, add lively dimensions to the participant's identity. The silhouette appears to be bursting with written information. This creates a free-flowing, almost poetic effect and combines reflective practice effectively with creative expression.

PMI – *Speaking or learning several languages can be confusing and interfere with learning English at an advanced level.* Conduct a PMI on this statement.

CAF – Think about all the things you love or admire about the languages you know and speak, and their related cultures. List these, then think again about what defines who you are. Try to consider what is less obvious, or anything you might have left out.

FIP – When you decide to learn a new language, what are the most important factors to take into account? (E.g. time, commitment, educational enrichment, future career plans, etc.).

Keywords: Maltese, Swahili, Japanese, Tagalog, identity

Figure 61. Madeline is a 22-year old female student who speaks two Chinese dialects (Teo Chew and Hainanese) at home, and learned Mandarin in Chinese school, Cantonese from her aunt., and Korean from TV.

Madeline is a 22-year old female student who speaks two Chinese dialects (Teo Chew and Hainanese) at home, and learned Mandarin in Chinese school, Cantonese from her aunt., and Korean from TV.

In her words

The head is in green (English) because I think and express myself in English. Teochew (the orange heart) links me to my grandparents and parents, and my heritage (Fig. 61). Hainanese (yellow) is my mother's native language, although I am not fluent in the language, I am making an effort to learn it because it is part of my identity. Cantonese (purple) is visibly smaller because it has never had much relevance in my life, but my parents wanted me to learn it. My parents enrolled me into Mandarin (black) school at a very young age and at the time I was too young to understand why it was relevant. However, on my last professional experience I was asked to act as a translator for my supervising teacher to a parent. So I want to improve my Mandarin proficiency.

Our response

Madeline mentioned the professional relevance of knowing a language, and this is becoming more important as Sydney is becoming more diverse. Students may only come to realize how languages might aid their careers later on in life.

Classroom application

Visual – A bold representation of colour can be a very satisfying way for participants to creatively express their heritage language identities. This, combined with symbolism can be encouraged to add further layers of meaning to the silhouette.

C&S – What careers have you considered for the future? Will learning another language besides English impact on your choices? Use a C&S to explore this.

FIP – When it comes to making decisions about which languages are most important for you to learn, how do you prioritise these according to their different purposes in your life?

APC – What language choices do you make when you spend time with your close and extended family, friends and others in the wider community? Discuss.

– Identify the avenues which generate the most possibilities for you to keep your heritage language and culture 'alive.' (Eg. personal, social and technology/media).

Keywords: Teo Chew, Hainanese, Mandarin, Cantonese, Korean, community language school

Figure 62. Neil is a 22-year old male student who speaks English and German at home, and learned Japanese in high school and Afrikaans from his partner.

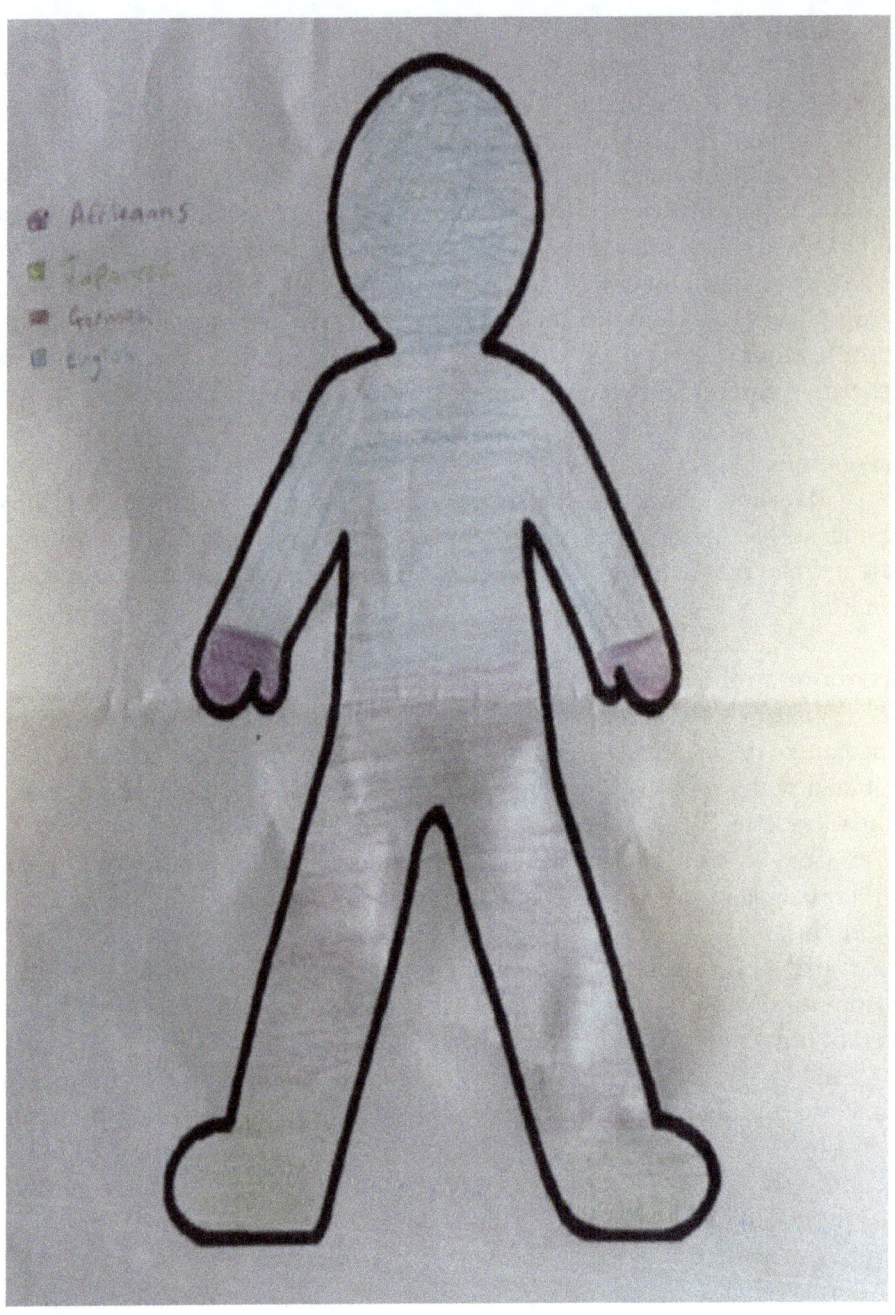

Neil is a 22-year old male student who speaks English and German at home, and learned Japanese in high school and Afrikaans from his partner.

In his words

English (in blue) is spoken by my father, brother and friends (Fig. 62). My mother was born in Germany and speaks German fluently with her relatives, both in Germany and Australia. I do not speak German but I have been in a context where this language is spoken all my life and that is why a large chunk of my silhouette is coloured to represent this. I studied Japanese for a year in high school but can now only recall general terms and statements. Finally, my partner was born in South Africa. Though she was not fluent in Afrikaans, the language is still part of my own personal experiences.

Our response

The importance of a language does not necessarily equate to proficiency. It may be more important to ask students to explore their emotional connection and their immersive environment.

Classroom application

Visual – Participants may represent language proficiency and usage relative to the size and parts of the body they colour in the silhouette. This might appear to be a simple way to illustrate these emotional connections, but can also reflect deeper analysis and evaluation of their importance. This could be useful for classroom discussion.

CAF – Does knowing your heritage language and learning other foreign languages mean you should be fluent in these languages? What other purposes can these languages serve in your life? (E.g. Emotional connections - family, extended family, friends and personal relationship; work relationships, academic enrichment, etc.)

CAF or C&S –
If you were to advise anyone on maintaining their heritage language or learning other foreign languages, what would you say?

Keywords: German, Japanese, Afrikaans, family

Figure 63. Diah is a 20-year old female student who speaks Bahasa Indonesia at home and learned Japanese and Arabic.

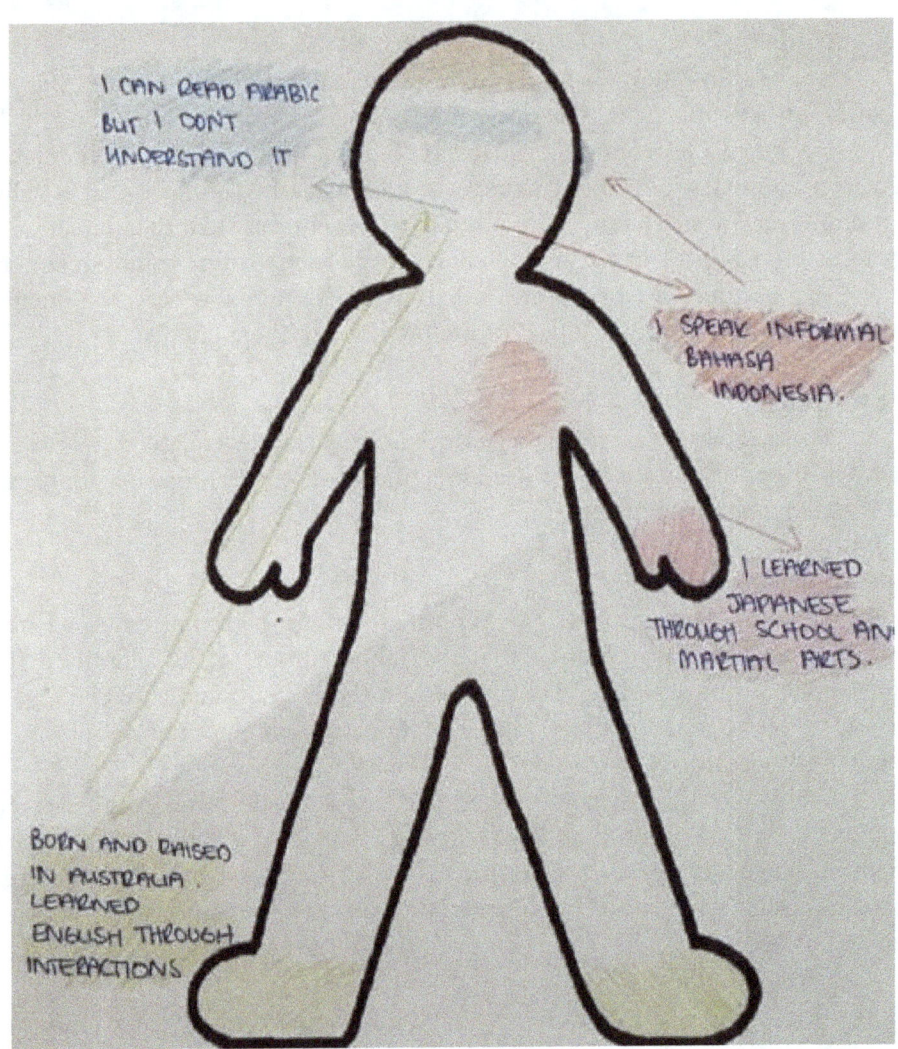

Diah is a 20-year old female student who speaks Bahasa Indonesia at home and learned Japanese and Arabic.

In her words

I chose green for English as I was born and raised in Australia, it is my home country therefore dominant language (Fig. 63). I coloured my feet green as I learned English through my experiences and interactions. I shaded my heart red to represent that Bahasa Indonesia is a language that I am connected to culturally. I learned Japanese through hobbies and school subjects, I coloured my hand pink. Finally, I coloured my eyes blue to represent that I can read Arabic. I have a spiritual connection to Arabic as it is a link to my religion.

Our response

Hobbies can motivate students to learn languages because having a hobby gives a personal context for a student to thrive in. This is especially true with popular culture, for instance, listening to pop music, watching TV drama, and playing video games.

Classroom application

Visual – The drawing relies on written explanations to connect ideas. This could initiate a useful classroom discussion to explore the different paths of learning and practising languages, such as co-curricular, extra-curricular and outside school settings.

APC – What are some of the alternative ways to learning languages outside the classroom?
– Identify the avenues which generate the most possibilities for you to keep your heritage language and culture 'alive'.

- Time spent with parents and siblings at home (personal)
- Interaction in neighbourhood community organisations and institutions (social and spiritual)
- Time spent with grandparents, extended family and friends (songs, cooking, memories, etc.)
- Communication via multimedia and different technologies (Facebook, Twitter, blogs, language apps, etc.).

Keywords: Bahasa Indonesia, Japanese, Arabic, travel

Figure 64. Simon is a 24-year old male student who speaks Dutch at home, but he also learned the language from a tutoring company.

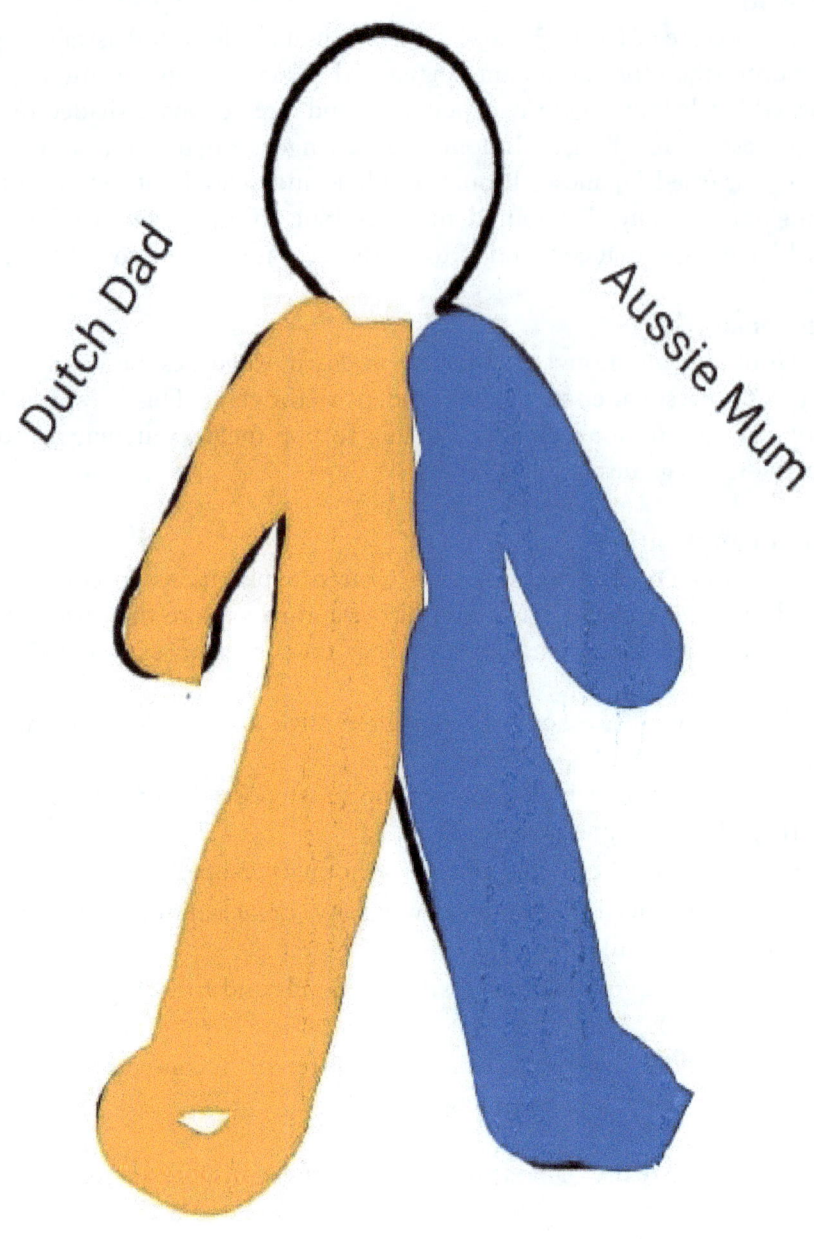

Simon is a 24-year old male student who speaks Dutch at home, but he also learned the language from a tutoring company.

In his words

My language silhouette (Fig. 64) is coloured in this way as the Dutch 'national colour' is orange (the football team is known as 'Oranje' (Orange), and the 'typical' white Australian associated colour is blue (also, this looked better than green and/or gold). I've labelled it clearly to show my Dutch heritage is paternal, and the Anglo heritage is maternal. I coloured each half equally as I do drift in and out of various self-identifications when it comes to language.

Our response

Sports can be a very powerful agent to encourage students to learn a language! It does not matter whether the learner is enjoying sports as a player or spectator, sports provides a good space for using a new language.

Classroom application

Visual – Colours dominate the silhouette which provide a simple, yet strong statement about the student's sense of identity. There are many ways to encourage students to creatively express their ideas, including technology. For example, teachers can introduce students to Microsoft Paint on Windows, free painting apps on their smartphones, or using touch-screen tablets.

PMI – It is possible to have more than one language and cultural identity? Use a PMI to discuss this statement.

– Sport is a great way to communicate. Use a PMI to explore this statement. (Could adapt this to other forms of communication, including music, dance, art, theatre, etc.)

AGO – How can knowledge of your heritage language be of value to you in your learning and social life? Consider this in terms of the goals you hope to achieve in the future.

Keywords: Dutch, identity, sports

Figure 65. Mattias is a 39-year old male student who speaks Polish, Russian, Hebrew and Yiddish at home.

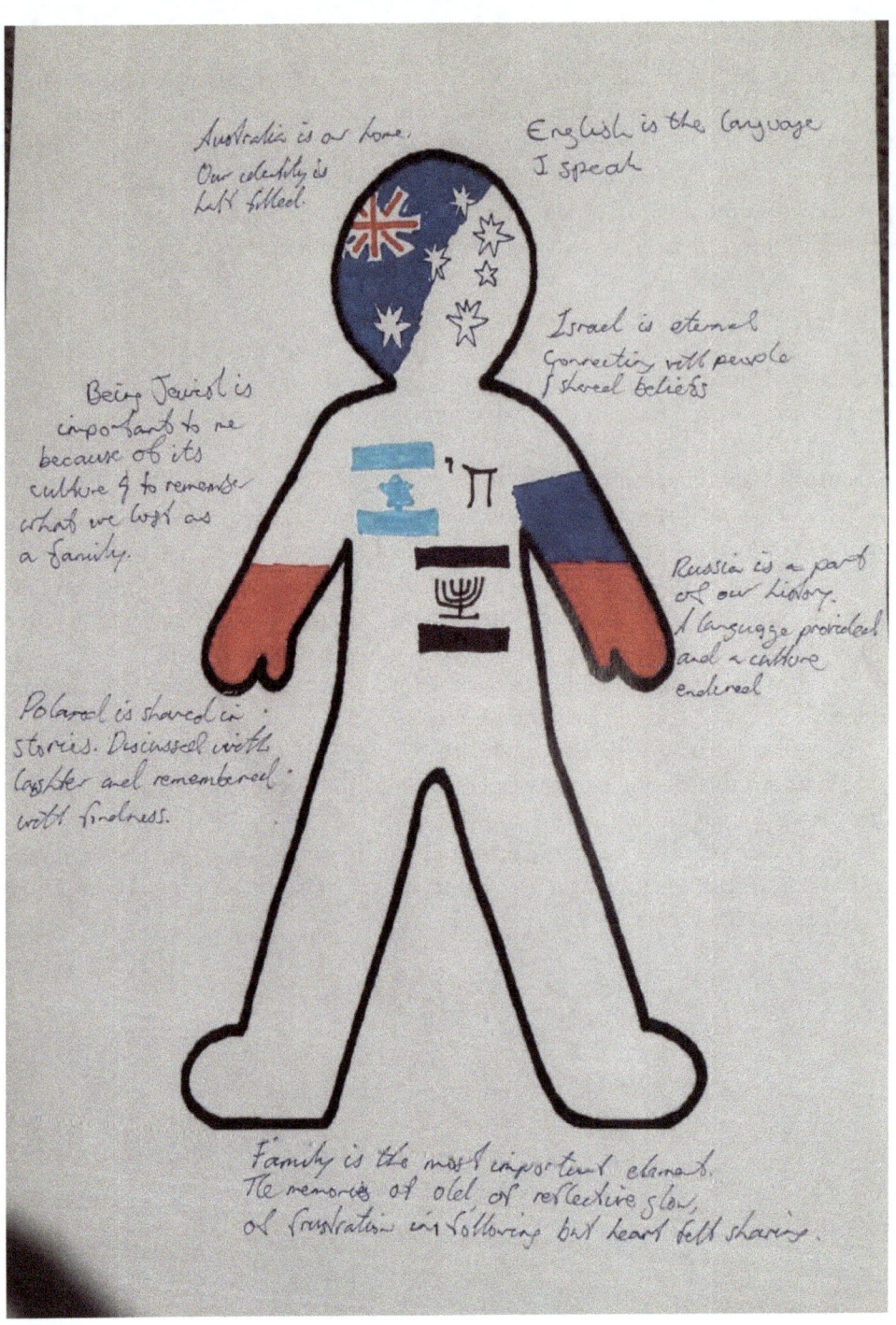

Mattias is a 39-year old male student who speaks Polish, Russian, Hebrew and Yiddish at home.

In his words

My heritage is important yet confusing to me (Fig. 65). Though the elements which make up my families past is important to me, it was confusing from a young age to hide it. My home only feels half full. I feel like something was left behind of my family.

Our response

The discussion of language and heritage can also be a difficult subject, especially with students from war-torn areas. But it is important for students to be able to express what they thought of the historical aspects of their heritage.

Classroom application

Visual – Strong symbolic and cultural representations show historical connections to the participant's diverse language and cultural backgrounds. Older students might include more complex written explanations and deeper expression of emotions. The intensity of feelings and memories related to heritage language and historical roots may not always be an easy area to address.

PMI – You see yourself as an Australian first, with English being the language you speak most of the time. Does this define who you are? Conduct a PMI on this.

C&S – How can the maintenance of your family history and the languages you are familiar with be of value to you in your future? (Consider family, friends, community, school, future career, etc.).

OPV – How has your own understanding of family history, past immigration and other related experiences affected the way you perceive others from different heritage backgrounds?

Keywords: Polish, Russian, Hebrew, Yiddish, family

Figure 66. Chivy is a 23-year female student with Khmer as her home language.

Chivy is a 23-year female student with Khmer as her home language.

In her words

The heart is coloured half blue and half purple because it symbolises how English and Khmer are a huge part of my identity, and it represents what languages I can fluently speak (Fig. 66). The reason I have traced my silhouette in blue (English) is because it represents my Australian nationality and that English is my first language and it is the language I use to communicate in almost every scenario. The flags in the speech bubbles represent the languages I know: English (Australia) and Khmer (Cambodia). The symbols inside my silhouette (traced in green) do not represent any languages, but they are Buddhist symbols. Coming from a Cambodian background, I grew up in a Buddhist household. Cambodia prides the Khmer language and Buddhism as part of their culture and identity. I personally believe that language, culture, and identity are linked together to shape our agencies. This is why I have drawn the symbols inside of the silhouette because it is personal and it reflects on my language identity as a Khmer person. This silhouette represents the way I project language, and the value of personal cultural identity within myself.

Our response

Many of our participants cited religious belief as a key aspect of their cultural and linguistic heritage. This may help us to have a better understanding of individual's language learning ecology. For one language learner, religion may be part of the ecology, for another it could be literature, or popular culture for another learner. By knowing learners' learning ecology, we will have better ideas on what may work and what may work even better in the classroom.

Classroom application

Visual – Symbols are used to represent Chivy's dual cultural and language identities. National flags indicate her external identity, while the Buddhist symbols are deeply held internalised beliefs connected to her spiritual beliefs. Silhouettes can act as effective tools for students to reflect on the more personal aspects of their lives which are most important to them.

CAF – We all connect with our cultural and language experiences in different ways. This might be through music, dance, art, literature, food, religion or the use of technology and media. Discuss some of these. Are there any other ways in which you choose to express your identity meaningfully?

AGO – What are your big dreams in life? Use an AGO to discuss some of these ideas and your goals for the future.

Keywords: Khmer, Buddhism, identity

CHAPTER 3

HOW CHILDREN DEPICT THEIR MULTILINGUAL SELVES? FROM A RESEARCH GOAL TO THE HERITAGE LANGUAGE CLASSROOM... AND BACK! A RESEARCH MEMOIR

Sílvia Melo-Pfeifer

University of Hamburg, Germany

At the beginning...

When I first started working with multilingual children and their drawings, I was far from imagining how diverse, heterogeneous and complex drawings of lived multilingualism would look. I started by designing a project meant to uncover images of languages and cultures that multilingual children deal with. More specifically, my main research goal was to understand the attitudes and beliefs bilingual German-Portuguese children developed towards Portuguese as a Heritage Language in Germany. Furthermore, I wanted to explore how their bilingualism related to the curricular multilingualism, i.e., with the languages they are in contact within the school context. In order to obtain a quantitative relevant amount of drawings, I then contacted *Portuguese as a Heritage Language* teachers in Germany and asked for their collaboration in the data collection process. I told them, they should collect the drawings in their classrooms, among children from 6 to 12 years old, following this instruction:

"Draw yourself speaking the languages you know."

I received an incredibly high number of drawings (almost 1000!) and a methodological question emerged: How should I analyse such a varied and extensive corpus of drawings?
In the following sections, I will explain the lessons I have learned from this project. They are a mixture of how I faced the problems during and after data collection, and analysis of alternatives to what I have done. These lessons should not be understood as a "to-do list", but instead as guidelines covering a range of alternatives and possibilities.

1. Before collecting the data

1.1 Be sure of your research goals, and reflect on all alternative data collection methodologies to achieve your goals

As I was about to start my research project, I asked myself how I could collect data on languages with children with limited written skills. Questionnaires, I thought, would not allow me to approach my target participants (at least not the younger ones). I thought of using interviews, but since I wanted to collect a representative amount of data, I also discarded this possibility.

Thinking of drawings as data collection, I started reading about this particular method and how to analyze the drawings. At the very beginning, I was quite sceptical about using drawings, because the available literature usually only reported on small number of drawings, in small case studies, and combining drawings with other data-collecting methods: interviews or text writing about the drawings. The question that is always raised is: How far can we be sure that the interpretation we make matches children's own interpretation and meaning? Again, I thought that drawings may not be the most appropriate method for my research project: I asked myself if a quantitative relevant data analysis would be possible resorting to drawings only. However, I was lacking alternatives and, more positively, I understood that drawings would allow me to access children's imagery and, with such an amount of data, I could perhaps look for tendencies, for common features, for shared representations attached to languages and cultures. And, since children could combine their drawings with written elements, I could also probably grasp the meaning of drawings through the interpretation of visual and written signs. So, I adopted a content-analysis perspective, analysing:

1. the diversity of elements attached to each language (paying special attention to Portuguese and German) and,
2. the frequency of different visual and written symbols attached to each language.

1.2 Make the instruction clear for everybody (and prepare yourself for the multiplicity of interpretations)

I thought that the instruction

"Draw yourself speaking the languages you know",

discussed with another colleague of mine, was clear enough and avoided unnecessary jargon: I was searching for a child-friendly instruction. I also wanted the instruction to avoid naming any language (so that children could include any language they thought of), language hierarchies ("the languages you like the most"), or, concurrence in skills possession ("the languages you know the best"). So, the chosen instruction focused the plurilingual repertoire of children as a whole, without focusing on any particular language and context. However, following some teachers' testimonies, children asked themselves the following questions: what is meant by "knowing a language"? Does "speaking" only relate to active production or is it possible to draw receptive skills? These questions are, of course, of foremost importance in my context, as children were mainly in contact with German and, as it happens to be common in heritage language speakers, the command of the heritage language is mainly oral and receptive. Some children asked if they were allowed to depict Portuguese, since they did not speak it 'well'.

Therefore, I had to be aware that teachers might have answered these questions differently and somehow influenced the final production of some children (or even of entire classes). Another feature I had to be aware of is the following: Since the data were collected in the heritage language classroom, it could be possible that Portuguese would be overrepresented, in order to fit perceived expectations.

1.3 Design a data-collection protocol

It is fundamental to design a data-collection protocol, if you are dealing with different stakeholders and contexts: it may ensure standard data-collection procedures. It may lessen the variability in the data-collection process and ensure some homogeneity and thus, the interpretation of the drawings as a (hopefully!) cohesive ensemble allowing data-comparability (for example, between rural and urban heritage language pupils). After data-collection protocol is established, be sure the participants in the data collection understand it, through personal exchanges (that is what I missed in my project!). Of course, if one is working alone, it may not be of extreme importance to have a detailed data-collection protocol.

A data-collection protocol could include:
- Instructions on what to say (for example, drawing task); how to accomplish the drawing task (paper and pencil, colour pencils, collage, ….) and the task duration; if pupils are to explain the drawing afterwards (through oral or written texts); and particularly, if they have to do it in front of the class, they should know it from the beginning.
- Parental authorization (particularly if there is personal data involved, even if anonymized);
- A following report on how the process was developed.

This final report may include the following sections (according to research choices):

- description of the class profile: How many children? Ages and "sex" distribution? Linguistic level?
- description of how children reacted and went on with the task: did they ask questions about the task or about the instruction?
- description of the atmosphere in the classroom: Was it playful or stressful? Were children laughing and commenting their drawings with their peers? Or were they anguished and sceptical?
- interpretations pupils/students voluntarily provided during or after drawing: Did they voluntarily ask for the teacher's attention to explain what they had drawn?
- students' feedback on their drawings (oral, written, both…), following the teachers' instructions: How many children presented their drawings? Which questions were asked by teachers? Could other children also ask questions? Could they comment on peers' productions?
- teachers' personal reports on their role and how they answered the questions raised during the task development.

1.4 Do not expect all drawings to fit your research goals

Even if this may sound discouraging, remember that not all children will interpret the drawing instruction the same way. Also, the children may attach different values to the task. Do not expect all of the drawings to fit your expectations and research goals. Nevertheless, as in any other data collection method, there are always valid and invalid collected data, incomplete answers or answers difficult to classify. In my case, about 80 drawings (out of about 1000) were not used in my research because I could not fit them in any research question I formulated.

2. After data collection

2.1 Classify the drawings

Working with a large sample made me realize I had to carefully classify all drawings, so that I could more easily access them. I resorted to folders to keep the drawings safe and protected. Other possibilities include the production of computer folders with the digitalised earlier versions of the drawings, or even the construction of a database with drawings classified by context, responsible teacher, age, school year, Portuguese proficiency, and so on.

2.2 Ask teachers for immediate feedback

When opting for the establishment of a protocol including teachers' feedback, it should be clear how soon they have to send it to you. Regarding my experience, waiting too long may cause teachers to forget some details. Since I did not design any protocol, I asked for feedback through e-mail responses.

It is also possible to construct a feedback questionnaire (paper or online) and send it to teachers immediately after the data-collection process. Being a more standardized feedback collection procedure, it can include open and closed questions and thus be easier and quicker to answer. Furthermore, if the research questions include aspects of teachers' roles, expectations and experiences, this feedback method allows for more structured data-collection.

3. During the analysis

3.1 Formulate a research question within the scope of the project goals

Depending on my research goals, I formulated different questions and I revisited the data for each one. Since my research focused on the attitudes and beliefs bilingual German-Portuguese children developed towards Portuguese as a Heritage Language, (but also German), in Germany and towards other languages (namely other heritage languages and languages of the school curriculum), I asked myself:

- How can I identify and describe pupils' social representations towards Portuguese and German languages?
- How do bi/multilingual children perceive their multilingual repertoires and depict the relationship between their languages?
- How are plurilingual selves and minds portrayed by children? Which plurilingual representations – interdependent or juxtaposed views of linguistic resources – are present in their drawings? Which are the most frequent?
- What are plurilingual repertoires of bilingual children made of (in terms of emotional dispositions, cognitive and verbal abilities, communicative skills and linguistic resources), and how do these children perceive and value themselves as plurilingual subjects?
- How are visual and written resources combined? (I called it "multimodal translanguaging" in a presentation)?
- How does Heritage Language Education contribute to the development of plurilingual and intercultural repertoires?

For each question, the corpus was revisited, redistributed and reclassified according to categories constructed in the scope of each theme.

3.2 Depending on the volume and the nature of data collected…

... Opt for a quantitative, qualitative or mixed-methods approach to data analysis. This means that the corpus may be explored by resorting to different analytical procedures, some more interested in grasping tendencies and commonalities by counting references (quantitative analysis), and others more interested in in-depth analysis of particular drawings or tendencies (qualitative analysis). Table 1 presents questions that may be asked resorting to the different analytical procedures, even if some questions may be answered resorting to a combination of both – the mixed-method approach:

Approaches to visual narratives analysis	
Quantitative analysis	Which languages are (more often) represented? Which symbols are attached to each language? Which are predominant? What kind of representations are attached to the different languages (affective, cognitive, …)? How are these representations distributed across languages? Does age or language proficiency influence the representations associated with languages? How are drawn and written elements combined? Do the two elements complement, supplement or contradict the meaning of each other?
Qualitative analysis	How are particular effects achieved through the combination of written and drawn elements? How are represented features sorted out and distributed on the page? If combined with verbal accounts of the drawings, which elements are more densely explained? Is the drawing explained as a metaphor, read as a whole or explained in detail, according to represented elements? How are relationships between verbal and/or visual elements explained?
Mixed-method approach	Mixture and dialogue between quantitative and qualitative analysis (for example, after a quantitative analysis, an in-depth description of particular features in the chosen productions).

The choice in my dealing with the drawings I collected depended on: volume of the data, particularities and commonalities identified across the drawings, possibility of categorization according to theoretical fundamentals, and research questions. Going back to my research questions (see 3.1), I usually resorted to a mixed-methods approach. Generally, I would classify the "valid" drawings (valid according to the research questions) according to theory-driven categories and explain the tendencies observed. I then described the particular features of drawings representative of the categories in more depth.

3.3 Go back to teachers if some doubts/problems persist and you need further information about the context

Asking teachers for support may be crucial if doubts persist or if complementary information on classroom or children's profiles are needed.

4. After the analysis

4.1 Be aware that your interpretation is but one interpretation

I am constantly asked how I can be sure that my interpretation is correct and to respect the meaning children wanted to transmit. Well, I am not. But I am sure that my interpretation is only a possible interpretation, as all interpretations are.

Even if children are called upon to interpret their drawings, the process of "semiotic transfer" – from drawings into words – may influence the content of the interpretation provided, simply because the resources are different. A question that I choose to think of is: Why should we more confidently rely on words rather than on drawings? Why are words easier to trust than other semiotic resources? Is it a sign of a "linguistic imperialism" on the research design and tradition?

In addition, the fact that children are not used to verbally reflecting on their languages may influence the quantity and the quality of the explanations they present. The same influence may be expected if children do the explanation task in a language they do not have a (perceived) good command of (as is the case of children with Portuguese heritage language explaining their drawings in that language). Another aspect that should be considered is that the explanation in front of the classroom by the teacher is always a co-construction of meaning, as the interpretation is (re)constructed according to the elicitation task, to the context (in my case, classroom context), to the audience and to the perceived goals of the task. Finally, there is a tendency to verbally reproduce explanations provided by peers that presented previously, somehow diminishing the spontaneity and the originality of individual verbal explanations.

So, we should keep in mind that explaining a drawing, even if by its author, orally or written, is always a dialogic process and concepts like "author intention" may be difficult (or even impossible) to grasp.

4.2 Rely on teachers and/or children as co-ethnographers to validate and/or co-interpret the drawings with you

This is something I have never done and that I am extremely curious about. Do my tentative interpretations fit the interpretations of the authors? Do the authors refute or confirm my readings? How can my interpretations influence the way the authors see their productions?

4.3 Share your analysis with other experts or researchers (namely if they come from other disciplines or school subjects)

A possible way to enrich the perspectives on drawings is to share the analysis with other researchers, even if they are not experts on drawings analysis. It may be very productive to share them with experts in the same area (in my case, multilingualism and heritage language education). Furthermore, colleagues in other research fields will probably pay attention to other aspects or details and thus enrich the analysis through a multi/transdisciplinary perspective.

4.4 Return to Phase 3 (data analysis) as often as you wish

New research questions can lead you to new analysis. Moreover, different angles of analysis may provide new insights to the corpus, enrich the scope of the project and raise the complexity and the accurateness of the (tentative) conclusions.

Further reading

Kalaja, P., & Melo-Pfeifer, S. (forthcoming, 2019). *Visualising multilingual lives: More than words*. Clevedon, UK: Multilingual Matters.

Melo-Pfeifer, S., & Simões, A. R. (Eds.) (2017). *Plurilinguismo vivido, plurilinguismo desenhado: estudos sobre a relação dos sujeitos com as línguas*. E-Book. Colecção "Encontros na Língua Portuguesa". Santarém: Escola Superior de Educação de Santarém.

Appendix 1. A Blank Portrait

INDEX OF KEYWORDS

Keyword	Figure number
Aboriginal languages	1, 35, 37
Afrikaans	62
Arabic	1, 5, 6, 15, 18, 21, 23, 25, 31, 47, 56, 53
Bahasa Indonesia	63
Bokmal	28
Bosnian	3
Buddhism	66
Bulgarian	51
Cantonese	2, 55, 61
Challenge	17, 49
Chinese	36
Church	20
Code-mixing	12, 18
Community language school	42, 46, 61
Conflict	25, 26
Creole	32
Croatian	36
Cuisine	23
Culture	34
Dari	48
Darug	37
Disadvantaged	26
Dutch	64
Emotion	7, 11, 15, 36, 40, 48
English	26
Family	3, 5, 7, 10, 11, 12, 14, 15, 16, 22, 24, 31, 32, 38, 40, 47, 55, 56, 57, 59, 62, 65
Farsi	23, 48
French	2, 4, 9, 13, 16, 19, 22, 24, 25, 28, 31, 32, 35, 47, 51, 56, 47, 59
Friends	19, 31, 32, 37, 47, 53, 54
Gaelic	16
German	11, 17, 24, 35, 38, 50, 58, 62
Gesture	3, 38
Grandparents	10, 14, 44

Greek	7, 39, 42
Hainanese	61
Hebrew	65
Heritage	1, 5, 10, 13, 15, 25, 28, 36, 38, 43, 44, 46, 47
Hindi	19, 29, 37, 44
Identity	2, 6, 19, 20, 21, 23, 30, 32, 39, 41, 43, 45, 46, 51, 52, 60, 64, 66
Italian	4, 14, 16, 19, 31, 35, 36, 39, 42, 44, 50, 57
Japanese	2, 12, 16, 19, 26, 27, 32, 33, 34, 38, 44, 52, 57, 60, 62, 63
Khmer	16, 66
Kirundi	9
Korean	2, 8, 19, 20, 31, 37, 61
Language known	1
Language loss	1, 9, 11, 13, 23, 33
Macedonian	46
Malay	6, 25
Maltese	14, 60
Mandarin	2, 19, 61
Migration	43
Music	31
Muslim	6, 25
Nepali	58
Norwegian	28, 33
Polish	33, 53, 65
Pop culture	19
Portuguese	59
Punjabi	5, 47
Romanian	54
Russian	28, 58, 65
School	24, 30, 35, 38, 56, 57, 58
Self-study	8, 24
Seychellois	32
Slang	40
Slovenian	16
Spanish	11, 16, 23, 30, 32, 36, 44, 49, 50, 54, 59
Sports	37, 64
Swahili	9, 60
TAFE	34
Tagalog	60
Tamil	43

Technology	30
Teo Chew	61
Thai	16
Travel	4, 8, 16, 19, 31, 32, 38, 50, 58, 63
Turkish	40, 44
Ukrainian	16
University	36
Urdu	5, 22, 37
Vietnamese	12, 16, 26, 27, 28, 41, 45, 52
Workplace	26, 27
Yiddish	65
YouTube	31

CANDLIN & MYNARD

Unit 1002 Unicorn Trade Centre
127-131 Des Voeux Road Central
Hong Kong

Other titles by Candlin & Mynard

Autonomy in Language Learning Series

Learning Japanese: Voices of Experience by Belinda Kennett and Yuriko Nagata
Autonomy in Language Learning: Opening a Can of Worms. Edited by Carol J. Everhard and Jo Mynard, with Richard Smith
Learner Autonomy in Second Language Pedagogy and Research: Challenges and Issues. Edited by Klaus Schwienhorst
Fostering Learner Autonomy: Learners, Teachers and Researchers in Action. Edited by Christian Ludwig, Annamaria Pinter, Kris Van de Poel, Tom Smits, Maria Giovanna Tassinari, and Elke Ruelens
Autonomy in Language Learning: Advising in Action. Edited by Christian Ludwig and Jo Mynard (forthcoming)
Autonomy in Language Learning: Stories of Practices. Edited by Andy Barfield and Natanael Delgado (forthcoming)
Autonomy in Language Learning: Getting Learners Actively Involved. Edited by Marcella Menegale (forthcoming)
Autonomy in Language Learning: The Answer is Learner Autonomy. Edited by Anja Burkert, Leni Dam and Christian Ludwig (forthcoming)
Autonomy in Language Learning: Tools, Tasks and Environments. Edited by Christian Ludwig and Jo Mynard (forthcoming)

Other

Stories and Storyline by Sharon Ahlquist and Réka Lugossy
Expatriate Families and Schooling in Japan: Issues, Challenges, and Experiences. Edited by Melodie Cook and Louise George Kittaka (forthcoming)
Women in Japanese Academia: Voices of Foreign Female University Teachers. Edited by Diane Hawley Nagatomo, Melodie Cook, and Kathleen Brown (forthcoming)

http://candlinandmynard.com